Columbus II
Ghosts

More Central
Ohio Haunts

Robin Smith

P.O. Box 1264, Worthington, OH 43085-1264
emuses@columbus.rr.com

Edited by Jennifer E. Poleon.
Design by Robin Smith.
Cover photo of Orton Hall by Randall Lee Schieber.
Ink-wash illustrations by Kathy Murphy.
Interior photos by Robin Smith except where indicated.

Contents

This one's for my dad, Robert Paul Beard, who set an example of curiosity and integrity that makes him
a hard act to follow.

Preface: Collecting Ghosts

"Do *you* believe in ghosts?"

If someone had given me a fifty-dollar bill for every time I've been asked that question in the past year, I'd be researching the Night Marchers on the Big Island of Hawaii this January instead of dealing with another central Ohio winter.

It's a fair question, and a hard one to answer. I've never *seen* a ghost. On the other hand, I've had several experiences with feeling "presences" and hearing my name spoken for which I could find no explanation. In my reading and research I run across many ghost stories that I simply can't accept at face value, either because they're so far over the edge or they're so nearly identical to dozens of other stories at similar locations. On the other hand, there are thousands of unspectacular little stories that ring true. Why bother making up a ghost that does nothing more interesting than look out a certain window or walk across a porch?

Another question, closely related but not quite the same, is "Do you really believe the people who tell you these stories?"

Many of the stories I find have been passed through many tellers—sometimes generations' worth. It's usually impossible to find anyone who has experienced the story firsthand. For those I look for corroboration in historical records and a certain consistency in accounts over the years. As for first-hand stories, I find that people who make up ghost stories out of whole cloth tend to a) make them a little too exaggerated and b) give themselves away in the telling. Most of the people who share their stories with me appear to be either unfrightened but sincerely puzzled about their experience or truly troubled about it in some way. Some tell their stories with an air of relief that someone doesn't think they're crazy. Do I believe their experiences? Since they're not *my* experiences, I can't say one way or the other — but I believe they are sincere in relating what *they* believe happened to *them*.

I believe that things happen every day that can't be predicted, replicated or explained by our current knowledge. Are some of those things actually encounters with disembodied souls? I hope so, but I don't have the answer. When asked, "Do you believe in ghosts?" my favorite answer is a quote from Shakespeare's *Hamlet*:

> There are more things in heaven and earth, Horatio,
> than are dreamt of in your philosophy.

I intend to enjoy the mystery.

• • •

One of the things that makes ghost stories so fascinating to collect is their universal nature. Sometimes it seems that every building, every corner, every tree hides a supernatural mystery. Those who have read my first book, *Columbus Ghosts: Historical Haunts of Ohio's Capital*, will remember that it was primarily historical ghost stories set in many of Columbus's landmark buildings. There are also several historic tales in this volume, but most of these stories are more contemporary first-hand accounts.

If you doubt the universality of ghost stories, consider that the sources of these stories include a firefighter, a hairdresser, a nurse, a witch, two highly regarded journalists, a teacher, a student, and a housewife; their ages vary from eighteen to mid-eighties. The settings include a turn-of-the-century firehouse, a community theatre, a modern suburban high school, a cemetery, a university library, and houses from the Victorian era to the late twentieth century. These people and places would appear to have nothing in common but the suspicion that they have experienced something supernatural — something beyond the realm of nature.

But have they? Many who study parapsychology and the paranormal believe that all human beings are born with the ability to apprehend things beyond the usual five senses: to predict events, to communicate without physical contact, to physically affect objects using only the mind, to see the spirits of the dead. These abilities become impaired as a child is told that they don't exist or that they are evil; by adulthood most of us have lost them, except for the occasional surprise glimmer.

In the future it is possible that these abilities, instead of being regarded as a gift or a curse, will be seen as perfectly natural.

I recently read a magazine article about Belleruth Naparstek, a traditionally trained psychotherapist who began her career at Cambridge Hospital, Massachusetts.* What makes Naparstek unique is that she freely speaks of having the ability to see others' auras and of often knowing what her patients' problems are before they tell her. This remarkable woman has used her abilities to help her create mind/body guided imagery exercises that are used by hospitals and surgeons across the country, paid for by insurance companies like Blue Cross/Blue Shield. Why? Because they *work*. Using the hidden abilities of patients' minds, these exercises help them to heal faster, to be more comfortable — and to save their insurance companies money.

It's a small step, but significant: fifty, thirty, even twenty years ago Naparstek and her guided imagery would have been considered psychic mumbo-jumbo.

Perhaps the future will bring a day when ghosts are accepted as a true phenomenon, not something in which to believe or not believe. I await future developments with curiosity.

* Michaud, Ellen, "Healing With Your Sixth Sense." *Prevention*, May 2003,
   pp. 154–161.

Acknowledgments

Grateful acknowledgment is more than due to the following:

Again, my business partners Jennifer Poleon and Kathy Murphy, whose support has been constant.

The many people who have shared their stories with me: Kim Shepherd, who not only invited me to speak to his creative writing class at Hilliard Davidson High School, but who generously shared his collection of Hilliard-area ghost tales; Susan Hudak, who volunteered stories about her parents' postmortem visits; Bill Hall of the Central Ohio Fire Museum, for giving a great tour of the museum and for tracking down the identity of Captain D; Jane Mixer and Joy Schmitt of the Little Theatre Off Broadway for tales of their theatre haunt; Mike Harden of the *Columbus Dispatch* and Fred Shannon, retired *Dispatch* photographer, for diametrically opposed comments on the Tina Resch poltergeist story; Charles Miller for leads on more stories than I could use in this book and for bringing Sally Brunner and the infamous Dr. Snook to my attention; Kara McVay of the Strand Theatre in Delaware for her theatre ghost stories and a fabulous flashlight tour into the bowels of the Strand; pseudonymous homeowners Leigh Sutherly and Tara Robinson — you know who you are; Tom Burns of the Perkins Observatory for his dramatic telling of Hiram Perkins' story; and Matt Androsky for sharing his encounter with Swamp Road Sally.

Thanks to Angee, Andy Henderson, Jim Willis and Troy Taylor for your shared interest and general encouragement.

And last but by no means least, thanks to my husband Brian and daughter Jessica, whose patience and forbearance are immeasurable.

Introduction

They're everywhere. In a conversation about haunted houses, Columbus-area psychic Deb Hinty once told me, "Everyone who lives in a house leaves their impression on it. All houses have ghosts, even new ones, because even if the house is new, someone else has lived on that land before it was built." I would extend that statement to include businesses, schools, parks, cemeteries — all the places we human animals touch during our lives.

Perhaps most of us are fortunate in that we are, for the most part, unaware of other planes of existence that parallel our own; of the presence of those who lived their earthly lives in our homes in years past; of long-dead souls who still strive to complete tasks left unfinished when their mortal lives were done. Yet how many have been touched occasionally by that other world? How many have heard their names whispered in an empty room? Have felt the touch of a human hand on their shoulder, only to turn and find no one there? Have felt a presence near them or have seen a person — wispy, smoky, transparent, or as solid as you or me — who suddenly wasn't there?

Ask your friends and family. You'll be surprised how many have had these unexplainable experiences one or more times in their lives.

Columbus and central Ohio have certainly not lacked for people and events to leave their ghostly traces here. The native Americans of the region, the early white settlers, the soldiers of the Civil War, businessmen and civil servants, heroes and villains — all are here, waiting to be sensed.

Welcome to haunted Columbus and central Ohio.

Who — or what — was the angry "spirit" that haunted the Resch household?

Tina's Angry Spirit

pol•ter•geist (pōl' tər gīst'), n. a ghost or spirit supposed to manifest its presence by noises, knockings, etc. [1840–50 < G *Poltergeist*, equiv. to *polter*(n) to make noise, knock, rattle + *Geist* GHOST]
—*Random House Webster's Unabridged Dictionary, Second Edition (1997)*

It began quietly enough: at 9 a.m. on Saturday,

March 3, 1984, the lights came on in the Resch household. All of them, simultaneously. John and Joan Resch called electrician Bruce Clagett, who was pretty sure they had a circuit breaker problem. After three hours, Clagett was stymied, unable to find any electrical problems or to make the lights stay off. Clagett even tried taping the light switches down; as soon as he walked away the lights would flip on again, with no one near the switches. By the time he left at 5:30, other strange things were happening. Small objects moved by themselves. The shower ran, though no one turned the faucets. Radios and the stereo switched themselves on — even when unplugged.

A "noisy spirit." The poltergeist is a special brand of ghost story. Stories of mysterious knockings and objects being thrown, moved or set on fire by unknown forces have been recorded since the Roman era. Always controversial, the poltergeist phenomenon has been "explained" as demonic manifestations, as involuntary psychokinetic activity, and in many cases, as outright fraud. In 1984, Columbus was host to what became one of the most famous poltergeist stories of modern times. Phantom or phony? The case still draws passionate responses from both sides.

By midnight Saturday, the Resches had called the Columbus police, but they could offer little help with the scene that greeted them — eggs splattered the kitchen ceiling, knives popped out of drawers and flew across the house, and furniture moved about. The disturbances seemed to be centered on the Resches' 14-year-old daughter, Tina, who was hit by several flying objects and followed around a room by a tumbling chair. The chaos continued Sunday, ceasing only when Tina left the house to go to church, and later to a friend's house.

Monday morning, Joan Resch called columnist Mike Harden at the *Columbus Dispatch*. Harden's October 7 column had been about Mrs. Resch's work as a foster mother to 250 children; he knew her to be a sensible, stable woman. She explained that she wasn't sure where to turn, that there were some very odd things happening at her house, and Harden agreed to drive up to the house on Columbus's north side.

When Harden arrived, he saw magazines sliding from an end table to the floor, untouched by human hands. As he watched, an afghan picked itself up off the floor and flopped onto Tina's head. Realizing he needed a photographer, he called the *Dispatch*, which sent veteran photographer Fred Shannon. Shannon quickly discovered that it was very difficult to capture the odd occurrences on film; the "force" seemed to avoid showing itself to the camera. Finally, Shannon outsmarted it: he prefocused his camera, dropped it to waist level and glanced away from Tina. Out of the corner of his eye, he caught a movement and tripped the shutter, capturing a photo of a phone

12

flinging itself across Tina's lap that was published in papers across the country.

Exhausted and desperate for an explanation, the Resch family moved to a motel, where Monday and Tuesday night passed quietly. They consulted with a neuropsychologist and neurologist, who was unable to explain the mayhem surrounding Tina Resch. The family returned to their home on Wednesday, hoping for the best — but as soon as Tina entered the house, objects began moving again.

A friend's family offered to keep Tina at their house overnight, and the Resches, who had previously withheld their last name in the newspaper reports, made the decision to hold a press conference at their home on Thursday afternoon and allow the media to observe "the force" for themselves.

The Thursday press conference began at 1:00; media film crews remained in the house until 9:30 that night. A cameraman for channel 6 in Columbus captured film of a lamp falling off a table that had clearly been knocked over by Tina herself, leading some to believe the Resches were staging a hoax. Tina's explanation was that she was tired and angry after having had cameras following her all day, and that she had finally given the crews what they wanted.

In spite of the lamp incident, others, including channel 6 reporter Drew Hadwal and photographer Shannon, maintained that they had seen other occurrences for which they could find no explanation — chairs moving in the kitchen when Tina was nowhere near them, glasses and mugs flying across the room. And no one had yet found an explanation for the electrical disturbances witnessed by electrician Clagett.

The Psychical Research Foundation in Chapel Hill, North Carolina expressed an interest in studying the phenomena. Director William Roll identified the Resches' problem as a possible case of recurrent spontaneous psychokinesis or RSPK, the ability to move or otherwise affect objects unconsciously. Individuals displaying this ability are typically adolescents who are under some emotional stress.

Tina Resch, 14, had been adopted by the Resches after she was deserted at 10 months of age. She had been frustrated in recent attempts to trace her birth mother, and told the press that she believed the strange happenings to be a punishment for her anger. The Resches agreed to let Roll and his assistant, clinical psychologist Kelly Powers, stay at their house to work with Tina.

From the other end of the investigative spectrum, the Committee for the Scientific Investigation of Claims of the Paranormal sent three members to Columbus: astronomer-physicist Steve Shore and astronomer Nick Seduleak from Case Western Reserve University in Cleveland, and James Randi, a New Jersey magician who had offered $10,000 to anyone who could show him a verifiable psychokinetic event. Mrs. Resch invited Shore and Seduleak to investigate after the Psychical Research Foundation team had left. However, Mrs. Resch refused to allow Randi into the house, fearing that he would sensationalize the case. The scientists refused to work without Randi, and contented themselves with interviewing various people who had observed the Resch phenomena. They also examined tapes and photos, including Fred Shannon's flying telephone. Having done so, the men announced that they were convinced the case was a hoax.

Meanwhile, the Resches turned down an offer of cash from the *National Enquirer* and a proposal for a made-for-TV movie, and received advice from hundreds on how to drive out the demons from their home, including suggestions that they throw out their Ouija board and Tarot cards (the Resches had neither in their home) and that Tina remove any posters of rock stars and rock and roll records in her possession.

After five days in the Resch home, William Roll suspected that Tina was indeed a victim of RSPK. The Resches sent Tina to North Carolina for further work with Roll in Chapel Hill. A month of psychotherapy and experimentation convinced Roll that he had seen real incidents of psychokinesis, including a candle that had moved across his living room while Tina's back was turned and a phone in a psychologist's office that flew at Tina from six to eight feet behind her. He also believed that Tina was psychic.

Tina Resch returned to Columbus and passed a relatively quiet summer, the chaos of the spring apparently over.

But the controversy continues. Was Tina Resch the center of a genuine case of paranormal activity? Or was she an unhappy girl acting out her anger in front of the world? Mike Harden, the *Columbus Dispatch* reporter who broke the story and kept in touch with the Resches over the years, has come to believe that there was nothing supernatural at work. At first he was confused by the things he saw and the stories he heard from Tina's family members. "Obviously it was a strange thing to encounter," he says. But shortly after the falling lamp was captured on film, Harden discovered that Tina Resch had not only read at least one book in which a character deliberately caused poltergeist-like activities, but had bookmarked passages describing the fake occurrences. "[Dr. Paul Kurtz from] CSICOP duplicated how she could throw the phone. You see something like that and it seems so strange. Then someone shows you how to do it," says Harden. "It's magic."

Fred Shannon, the now-retired *Dispatch* photographer, adamantly disagrees. "I know damned well what I saw," he says. "I would swear over my mother's grave that this happened." Shannon sensed an intelligent force behind the phenomena. When he took that famous phone shot, he and a reporter from Florida had been watching the phone moving for some time, but as soon as he tried to capture it on film, it stopped. "I sat there for what must have been close to 10 minutes with my camera to my eye. Then Tina's stepbrother walked into the room and I turned my head to see who had walked in. As soon as I turned away — zing! — there went the phone." Shannon and the force continued their otherworldly staredown until Shannon successfully faked disinterest. The force "blinked" — and Shannon caught the phone in full flight.

Shannon also saw many other incidents that defied logic. "There was a lemon tree inside the front door," he says. "The lemons would come off that tree and fly down the hall and *around a corner* into the room where we were sitting. Now how do you explain that? *Wires?*"

"People want to be convinced," says Shannon. "I don't try to convince people anymore. I know what I saw."

Two thoughtful men, both witnesses to the events as they occurred; two diametrically opposed opinions on what really took place. After nearly twenty years, the Resch poltergeist still has the power to polarize.

What do *you* think?

Can the habits of a lifetime continue — even in death?

Photo illustration by Robin Smith

Through a Glass, Darkly

On May 9, 1974, 16-year-old Susan Neff came
home from school and found her father, Wayne, dead in his bedroom
at their home in Whitehall. "He'd worked at Buckeye Steel all his
life, and had lung problems from that. He had apparently had a
coughing fit in the bathroom that caused him to hemorrhage. He
made it to his bed before he died. It was pretty gruesome," she says.

Wayne Neff was dead — but not gone, according to Susan. After
her father's death, Susan and her mother, Dorothy, frequently smelled
cigarette smoke in the house, though neither smoked. Both suspected
that it was Wayne, lingering in the home where he had drawn his last
breath. But there were other, more frightening incidents to come.

Susan moved out of the house when she turned eighteen. Her
older brother Mike and his wife Lenia then moved in with Dorothy
Neff and her not-quite-departed husband. About a year after Wayne
Neff's death, Lenia had her own experience with his spirit.

"My dad was an alcoholic," says Susan. "During the times when
he was 'straight'" — she provides quote marks with her fingers — "he
would spend a lot of time in the basement, because he had a little
stash of liquor down there in a footlocker. He had a workbench and a

shower and sink down there, with a mirror so he could shave, right next to the washer and dryer." One afternoon Lenia Neff went down to the basement to do laundry. As she turned away from her work, she glanced at the shaving mirror — and saw her father-in-law's face looking back at her. "She flew up the stairs," says Susan.

One evening all three Neffs went out, turning off the lights before leaving. When Mike returned to the locked house, he found the lights on in his father's old bedroom, though he was positive they had been out when he left. More chilling, however, was the phone, which had been on the bedside table. Now it lay on the bed, with the receiver off the hook as though it had been tossed or dropped.

The incident that most troubles Susan also took place while the Neffs were out. "I still get goose bumps when I think about this," she says. "My dad used to pull a kitchen chair over to the counter. He'd sit there and lean on the cabinet with a cigarette and a drink. A lot of times he'd fall asleep there. We had cigarette burns on the carpet from him sitting there all the time."

Late one night the Neffs came home to find one of the kitchen chairs moved. The chair, which had been pushed up to the table with the others when they left, was pulled up to the kitchen counter, just where Wayne Neff had left it so many times during his life.

One might think that one ghostly parent would be enough to deal with, but Susan believes her mother also visited her after her death. Dorothy Neff died on March 28, 1999, after a lengthy stay in a nursing home. She was 82 years old, and lucid to the end.

About four months after Dorothy's death, Susan woke during the night. She looked up at the ceiling fan over her bed and saw sparkling lights hovering around the ceiling fixture. "They looked like little Christmas tree lights," she says. As she watched, the lights gathered into a group and flew out the window. "I don't know if I'd call it my mother's ghost or not, but I've always thought it was her energy somehow."

A more poignant occurrence took place about two months later. "I woke up because I thought I heard the telephone ring," she says. Susan picked up the phone and heard her mother say, "Just calling to say hi!"

"I yelled at her not to hang up," says Susan, "but she was gone."

Susan is still not sure if she actually heard the telephone ring or even if the experience was an extremely vivid dream, but of one thing she is certain: Her mother's voice spoke to her. "I didn't want her to hang up," she says, blinking back tears. "I really wanted to talk to her."

Who is the mysterious presence at the Little Theatre Off Broadway?

The Ghostly Piano Player

Harvey, the classic comedy about Elwood P. Dowd and his invisible rabbit companion, is a favorite at the Little Theatre Off Broadway. And why not? Harvey probably feels right at home with the *other* invisible inhabitant of this Grove City community theatre.

Joy Schmitt, Director of Junior Theatre, and Jane Mixer, currently the group's Trustee, have both been with the Little Theatre Off Broadway since long before the group moved into their current home. "I think I've been everything but treasurer at one time or another — I'll do anything but handle the money!" laughs Schmitt. Both have had odd experiences in the theatre. Mixer says she's heard unexplained footsteps and odd sounds many times. A favorite story concerns an actress who left the hat she wore in *Harvey* on a particular chair, so she would know where it was at performance time. One night she reached for the hat and it was gone — but there was another there in its place. The show went on with the substitute hat. No one ever owned up to making the switch ... no one human, at least. But Mixer defers to Schmitt when it comes to brushes with the supernatural at the Little Theatre Off Broadway.

23

Schmitt doesn't like mysteries. She likes explanations. She wants reasons for the old building's odd creaks and mysterious sights. She doesn't always find them.

"This is an old building," she says. "It's full of noises. When I hear or see something strange, I look for a logical explanation. Sometimes there just doesn't seem to be one."

Located on the west side of Broadway in Grove City, the Little Theatre's neat brick building houses a colorful history. The Kingdom Theatre was built in 1916 by a Mrs. Koening, who later anglicized her name to King in reaction to anti-German sentiment from World War I. The theatre provided Mrs. King's blind daughter Ethel with an opportunity to use her talent for playing the piano. As silent movies played at the Kingdom, Mrs. King prompted her daughter with whispered cues: fast music for a chase scene... a sad theme for a tragic event... a playful jig for comedy.

The Kings sold the theatre in 1927. In 1955 the theatre was purchased by Our Lady of Perpetual Help Catholic Church, which met there for two years until their building was completed. After the church moved into its new quarters further north on Broadway, the building reopened as the Douglas Theatre in 1959. When the Douglas Theatre closed in 1968 the Little Theatre Off Broadway group, which had been performing in local schools, signed a rental agreement with an option to buy on the building.

What they found was a run-down, dirty movie theatre with gum on the seats and popcorn glued to the floor, but the group jumped in, cleaned up and mounted the first production in their new home in December of 1968. The building's first carpeting came from the recently-closed JCPenney store in downtown Columbus, ripped up piece by piece from the old store and reinstalled at the theatre. Seating was improvised and included church pews and various types of chairs, but the theatre quickly became a lively local haunt. Literally.

One evening in October of 1978, Schmitt was alone in the theatre. She sat down in the first row of the auditorium, right in front of the stage. Suddenly, "There was a horrendous crashing sound from above me. It was awful. It really scared me." Seeking the source of the noise, she checked the front area of the theatre, thinking that perhaps it was windy outside and one of the doors had blown open. The doors were locked, the wind still. There was no one upstairs, no one else in the front of the building. Venturing back into the auditorium, she again sat down in the front row. Again, the crashing noise came from above. Again, she checked the doors and the rooms upstairs. Again, she found nothing to account for the noise.

Two days later, disaster struck. Fire broke out in the building, racing from the front of the stage area up the ceiling to the technical booth in the rear of the auditorium. Richard Lawson, then LTOB president, was alone in the building, having stopped to pick up a costume that needed cleaning. The fire nearly trapped him in a restroom; he escaped by wrapping his coat around his head and staggering through the smoke-filled building to the front door. In 10 minutes, the auditorium was a ruin, filled with collapsed paneling and charred ceiling pieces. The intense heat from the fire melted the plastic controls and equipment in the tech booth and destroyed lights worth thousands of dollars.

The timing of her experience left Schmitt wondering if there was a connection. "In hindsight," she says, "I wonder if maybe it was some kind of warning."

Miraculously, the floor, roof and walls of the burned theatre were found to be structurally sound. Determined to begin again, the Little Theatre Off Broadway continued their season in borrowed quarters. The group once more set about cleaning and renovating the building that they had bought outright from the Catholic Church — making them one of only a few Columbus-area community theatres to own their own building. Today the theatre is a cozy place with neat rows of comfortable (matched) chairs in the small auditorium. As with most theatres, the building is a maze of passages and rooms. The original basement at the front of the building, which requires stooping by anyone taller than four feet, connects with a newly-dug area under the stage where new dressing rooms are being built. Between the front doors and the auditorium, a set of steep stairs is hidden by a curtain. At the top of these stairs are three rooms. To the right is the tech room, with plexiglass windows overlooking the auditorium and filled with lighting and sound equipment. Straight ahead is another room that also overlooks the auditorium, now occupied by a costume rack. To the left is a small storage room. Above the tech rooms and auditorium is a large open space which is currently not used.

Lots of room for an enterprising ghost to wander. Since the mysterious overhead crashes, Schmitt has had several other close encounters of the weird kind.

Late one night, Schmitt and several others held a meeting in the auditorium. The group sat at the front of the seats at stage right. As the group talked, they heard the distinctive sound of the backstage door slamming shut. Hard. Two pairs of men from the group circled the stage in opposite directions, looking for an intruder. "We thought it was a vagrant," says Schmitt. "We had had one get in once before and thought maybe he'd gotten back in somehow." Finding nothing amiss, the four men met up in front of the backstage door. It was locked from the inside by a heavy hook-type lock that requires the door to be pulled tightly closed to be set in place. No one came across the stage. No one was behind the stage. So who slammed the door — and then took the time to lock it?

Another night Schmitt and another LTOB member, Rich, were shutting up the building. Schmitt was standing near the bottom of the steep staircase to the tech room. The lights were off upstairs and the stairway curtain had been pulled closed; she had just turned out the downstairs lights when she heard heavy, definite footsteps coming down the stairs. The footsteps stopped just behind the curtain. "They were very clear, very heavy," she says. "But just to be sure I wasn't hearing things, I looked at Rich and said, 'Did you hear that?'" He had. Schmitt cautiously opened the curtain. The stairway was empty, the upstairs dark. "I asked Rich if he wanted to go upstairs and check around, and he said 'No!' So I did." There was no one there.

The tech room stairway is also the only place Schmitt has actually seen the LTOB ghost — or at least a part of her. Walking past the stairway one day, she looked up and saw the bottom part of a long dress or skirt disappear into the left storage room. "It looked like the back part of the dress, the part that would be pulled behind as someone walked past," she says.

Although Schmitt has never seen more of the ghost than her hem, she was present in the building when someone else did. Scott and Julie were working in the tech booth that night. While looking out into the darkened auditorium, they both noticed the reflection of a woman in the plexiglass window, as if someone were standing in the doorway at the top of the stairs. The woman wore a high-necked blouse or dress with a brooch at her throat, and her face was clearly reflected in the window — except for the area around her eyes, which was dark, as though heavily shadowed. When they turned to see who was there, the doorway was empty.

It was the reflected woman with the shadowed eyes who caused the Little Theatre members to speculate that perhaps their ghost was Ethel King, the blind pianist whose mother built the theatre as a place for her daughter to perform. "We don't know for sure that it's her," says Mixer, "but we do have an entity here."

"And wouldn't it make sense that it would be Ethel?" asks Joy Schmitt. "This place was built for her. This is her home."

Not all of the earlier occupants of Delaware's Northwest Historic District have moved on.

We're Here. They're Here.

Leigh Sutherly* and her husband Max* live in a warm, homey-looking brick house in Delaware's Northwest Historic District. They've been there for several years, but among the house's occupants, they are definitely the newcomers.

"We noticed right away after we moved in that the house was really noisy," says Leigh. There were frequent bumping and thumping noises, and sometimes the sounds of objects falling. "At first we blamed the noises on the cats. We also sometimes found the heat turned up really high, but didn't really think too much about it. Then the bathroom faucets started turning themselves on. That was when we knew we had something going on."

"Sometimes we'd come home and find the heat turned up to like 95 degrees," says Leigh. "Things were moved around. We started finding hairpins lying all over the house. No one in our family uses hairpins. One night we were all sitting at the table eating dinner and the downstairs bathroom faucet came on."

By now the Sutherlys were convinced that they had an invisible roommate, but who? A possible answer came when they remodeled the downstairs bathroom.

"I was working in the bathroom and had the feeling that someone else was there watching me," says Leigh. "I turned and saw a woman in the doorway. She was wearing a blue flannel robe, one of those old-fashioned ones with the striped trim around the lapels." Not particularly frightened, Leigh had the impression that the woman was just curious about what she was doing.

A few days after the mysterious woman's appearance, Leigh was talking to a neighbor and described some of the odd things happening in the house, including her spectral visitor. "I'll bet that's Helen," said the neighbor.

Helen was a professor at Ohio Wesleyan University who lived in the Sutherlys' house for thirty years. "She was always cold. She kept the heat turned way up and sometimes called the gas company to ask them to send her more gas," says Leigh. No word about whether Helen used hairpins.

One ghost per household might be enough for most families to deal with, even a peaceful professorial sort like Helen. But the Sutherlys have other company from beyond in their home, as well.

Tobey,* a childhood friend of Leigh's, came to visit a few years ago with her children. Tobey has been sensitive to ghosts since she was a young girl, and soon discovered another resident in the Sutherly home. "Tobey came downstairs and asked me if I knew I had a ghost on the second floor," says Leigh. "She described him as an adolescent boy, and as angry or frustrated about something. She didn't like him; he made her very uncomfortable, and she won't stay in my house any more."

During the same visit, Tobey felt the presence of a slave hiding in the pantry. "He's kind of cowed down back in the corner like he's trying to hide," says Leigh. What Tobey was not aware of at the time is that Delaware was very active in the Underground Railroad. Perhaps the unfortunate slave's fear has held him here long after his body passed on.

Now the owner of a business in downtown Delaware, Leigh is a very down-to-earth, grounded woman, but she has no doubts that there are many more things in this world than we see with our eyes. A nurse for many years, she has dealt with dozens of dying people in her lifetime. "Most people are OK when they go, but sometimes you would have a patient who was really afraid to die, who really fought it. There was one man I remember who was absolutely terrified to let go and hung on long past when he should have died. After he finally passed away, every one of the nurses saw him somewhere on the floor. He just didn't want to go."

Her house's "other" occupants don't frighten her. Helen seems harmless enough — just curious about the other folks in her home and their activities. The slave ghost stays in his corner, not interacting with the living people who come and go.

Leigh has never seen the boy upstairs. "He can be very noisy. I have the impression that he wants to scare people, but he can't really pull it off except with younger kids. I think he has something he wants to say and can't figure out how to communicate it, and I don't know how to help him." Does it worry her that Tobey dislikes the ghost to the point of not staying in the house? "No," says Leigh. "He's a kid. He's frustrated. He doesn't threaten me."

"They're here. We're here. It's OK," she says.

Captain Dukeman still awaits the call of the fire bell at Engine House 16.

The Ghostly Captain Dukeman

Firefighters live and work on the edge of the precipice, doing a job that could make any day their last. Like police officers and medical personnel, they are confronted with life—and with death—on a daily basis. Though necessarily a practical and down-to-earth group, many firefighters will also admit to brushes with the unexplainable. Call it a hazard of the job.

Captain George Noah Dukeman was a 52-year veteran of the Columbus fire department when he died on April 16, 1939. He joined the department on March 1, 1887 at the age of 20 and was described in his obituary in the *Columbus Dispatch* as "a veteran of every major fire [in Columbus] after 1890." Promoted to lieutenant in 1892 and to captain in 1897, he was cited for bravery several times, the first time in 1916 for rescuing Mrs. Estella Brunning from the fourth floor of the burning Savoy Hotel at Gay and Fourth streets, and again in 1917 for assisting in the rescue of a woman and two men from a fire on East Long Street. Death found Dukeman after a three-month sick leave—his only sick leave in 52 years.

Captain Dukeman spent 30 years as the captain of the No. 8 Truck Company, based at Engine House No. 16 at Fourth and

Chestnut streets. Dukeman's tenure there began when the building was completed in 1908—the last firehouse in Columbus built to accommodate horses. The front of the first floor consisted of three equipment bays. Along the back wall were 11 doors, 10 leading to horse stalls and one door in the center for the firemen to enter the stable area. The stall floors were constructed of wood block for the comfort of the Percheron horses used to pull the equipment. Above the stable area was the hay loft, with a trap door for dropping the hay down to the first floor to feed the horses. The front half of the second floor consisted of the large dormitory room where the men slept, with two separate rooms for the officers, two locker rooms, two washrooms, and a

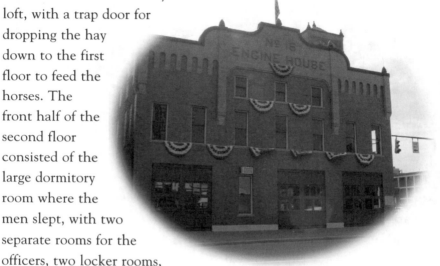

Death has not interrupted the Captain's vigilance.

common room. On the south side of the building was a 50-foot-tall bell tower, which not only housed the bell used to call firefighters to the station, but was used as a drying area for cloth fire hoses.

An ingenious system for getting the horses hitched to the equipment allowed the firemen to get a pumper on its way in as little as 45 seconds from the time the alarm bell rang. When an alarm was received from a call box, the central dispatcher rang the bell at the nearest station in a pattern that told which box the alarm had come from—for instance, one long and two short rings for box twelve. The electrical signal to the bell also tripped wires that opened the station's front doors and the horses' stalls. The highly-trained horses quickly

34

took their stations in front of the equipment, where the driver pulled a rope lowering their harness into place. The horses' collars were specially designed with hinges at the top so they would come down over the animals' necks and gravity would cause them to close and latch; all the firemen had to do was check that the latches had closed completely. It was, and still is, a point of pride for firefighters to respond to an alarm with speed and efficiency.

The stories passed down to the firefighters at Engine House 16 describe Captain Dukeman as a stickler for detail and a man who insisted on equipment being kept in good condition and at the ready, whether horsedrawn or, after the last team of horses was retired from the department in 1919, motorized. He was known to keep a sharp eye on the engines and to walk the second floor rooms at all hours, checking the locker rooms to make sure all was in good order.

Those stories also say that Captain Dukeman, affectionately called "Captain D," still walks in Engine House No. 16.

Renamed Engine House 1 in 1953, the station at Fourth and Chestnut remained in active use until 1981, and generations of firefighters experienced the mysterious footsteps that echo on the stairs and across the second floor. "That's Captain D," rookies who asked about the footsteps were told. "He's just checking the equipment again." The captain apparently had some companions to share his eternal vigil. Although the last horses at the station retired more than 80 years ago, firefighters were occasionally startled to hear the snorts and restless movements of the mighty Percherons in the stall area. Sometimes the creaking of leather harnesses was heard, or the loud clank of a heavy hoof impatiently striking the metal-encased stall doors that sprang open at the sound of the alarm bell; like Captain D, the horses remained eternally ready to spring into action.

A new Engine House 1 was built in 1981, a block north of the old station. In 1983 a non-profit group of Columbus firefighters obtained a 99-year lease on the old engine house, hoping to build and operate a fire museum and learning center. Old photographs were used to return the building's exterior to its original appearance, and extensive renovations were completed on the first floor. In October 2002, the Central Ohio Fire Museum and Learning Center opened its doors to the public. The equipment bays are filled with restored antique fire-fighting equipment, including an 1881 Amoskeag steamer similar to the steamers pulled by the horses who once made their homes in the building. There is a kids' area where future firefighters can slide down a brass pole and operate the lights, siren and horns in the cab of a modern fire truck. The old stall doors have been restored, complete with the dents made by dozens of powerful hooves, and a model horse stands in a rebuilt stall, gazing out his open door. The rear of the stable area has been turned into a learning center for children where firefighters can demonstrate a child's room filling with smoke and a firefighter searching the darkened room using an air bottle and face mask. Another area shows the dangers and proper handling of kitchen fires.

Bill Hall, president of the Central Ohio Fire Museum, is also an active firefighter and Emergency Medical Technician and the Columbus fire department's historian. Hall is obviously proud of how far the museum has come in the 20-plus years since restoration began. He also occasionally worked out of the old building and knows its history well. "We still hear sounds in here we can't explain," he says. "Mostly it's footsteps on the stairs or on the second floor"—which is now empty, awaiting further restoration work. "Sometimes we'll come in in the morning and find lights on that weren't on when we left the night before." There are other electrical glitches, as well. "The toaster in the kitchen-fire demo area sometimes refuses to turn off. We switch it off, and a second later it comes back on. I don't know if that's the ghost or not, but we sure haven't found any reason for it. We have to unplug it to make it stay off."

Hall and the other volunteers and board members who work in the building accept the idea that they may be sharing their building with something they can't see, and it doesn't trouble them even when their ghostly lodger gets a little rambunctious.

One memorable incident occurred over Thanksgiving weekend in 2001. The museum includes a second building behind the old engine house, which was built a few years after the main structure and housed a maintenance and testing area for the equipment. It also has a second-floor hayloft where additional feed for the horses could be stored.

A volunteer who had come in to work in the museum over the holiday weekend noticed that the hayloft door on the second floor of the shop building was open, swinging in the wind. A board member was called to enter the building to check and re-lock the door.

The door is closed on the inside by a sturdy lock, so it is extremely unlikely that it could come open by accident. No one had been working in the rear building recently. So how did the door get opened? "We don't know," says Hall. "There was no reason for the door to be open and there's no way it just came open by itself. But there it was."

Evidently Captain D remains vigilant, holiday or no. Maybe he just wanted to spread a little holiday cheer — and a little extra hay — to his ghostly equine companions.

The scary stories at the Strand are not all on-screen.

The Haunting of the Strand

The areas of Delaware's Strand Theatre that the public never sees are a treasure trove of old theatre equipment, furniture and the miscellany that collects in old buildings. Behind the perforated movie screen in the main auditorium and in the dark areas upstairs lurk antique projection and sound equipment, film magazines from the days of flammable nitrate film, old furniture and doors, even plumbing fixtures from the twenties and thirties.

Among the hodgepodge of equipment and memorabilia, there also lurk several less ... *tangible* occupants.

Kara McVay, who manages the Strand for owner Ohio Wesleyan University, has a long history with the theatre. Has she ever seen a ghost there? "Oh, yeah," says McVay. "I got run out of here last Friday night. I was standing by the concession stand after closing and looked out into the lobby, and there he was" — he being an entity she refers to as "the mean ghost." "We don't know who is is. He's male, and not friendly. I saw him standing by a pillar, with his arms crossed and looking like this." McVay makes a grim face. "I left."

McVay worked at the Strand for the previous owners, George and Cindy Johnson, for five years from 1986 to 1991. In August of 2002 she returned as the theatre manager. Her love for the theatre is obvious as she shows off objects such as original cast iron seat ends and the ornately decorative backstage radiator that still provides the heat for the main auditorium. "The theatre was built in 1916 as a vaudeville house," she says. "The east section of the building — the concession area and the side auditorium — were not originally part of the theatre. That section was built in 1908 and a later owner punched through the separating wall and added the auditorium. The main part of the theatre has operated continuously since it was built." Walking through the main seating area, she points out the original decorative plaster work. "When I worked here in the eighties, all the weird stuff was pretty much backstage and upstairs. Since then the ghosts seem to have moved out into the auditorium and lobby also, but you really have to see the back parts of the place to understand how it could be haunted."

Like all theatres, the Strand is a maze of hallways, storage areas, projection booths and dressing rooms; a flashlight is a necessity as well as a comfort in the dark passages. The area behind the screen is used for storage; at one end of the space is an opening into the area that housed the pipes for the original theatre organ, now empty except for a small wooden box too heavy for McVay to pull out of the space. "I don't know what's in it," she says. "Could be anything."

Up a flight of stairs on the other side of the stage is a small room where the theatre pianist provided the "sound track" during the days of silent movies. The pianist watched the action on-screen through an ornate plaster screen, still in excellent condition.

The third floor of the main theatre was once dressing rooms; today the old washroom and one dressing room are filled with old parts and fixtures and the other two are filled with air-conditioning equipment. "This is where we never came alone when I worked here in the eighties," says McVay. "You had to come up here every day to turn on the AC, and it was really bad. It always felt like there was somebody behind you, and your hair kind of stood up—you know that feeling? Even the guy who works on the AC equipment doesn't come up here by himself. He says his hair stands on end the whole time he's up here."

The balcony area of the old theatre is now a separate auditorium with its own screen. "The activity up here seems to be all in the projection booth," McVay says. "This is where I smell [former owner] Cindy's Skin-So-Soft lotion sometimes when I'm cleaning up. And sometimes this door seems to lock itself from the inside. I think that's Cindy, too. She was always one to play pranks when she was here."

She demonstrates the hook-and-eye lock, which takes some force to fasten. "There's no way that's going to lock accidentally. There's another way in, but it's a real pain because you have to go way out around through the other building to get here."

The other exit leads into the upper story of the east building, once apartments. The rooms are now a jumble of old movie posters, furniture, doors, scrap wood and ductwork. With the windows board-ed over, the space is very dark and—mostly—very quiet. "It can be very noisy up here sometimes, especially at night," says McVay. "This is another area I don't go into alone." Parts of the floors are still covered in linoleum designed to look like floral carpets, and pieces of calendars from the 1950s hang on the walls. Perhaps the owners of those calendars still drop in to check their schedules.

Also on this floor is projection booth 3, which serves the side auditorium and is one of Rodney's haunts. Rodney was McVay's cousin, who worked at the theatre during the early seventies and died in a house fire in 1987. Rodney plays tricks with the projection equip-ment. "This projector came to us brand-new, still in the box," says McVay. "But we have all kinds of little problems with it that should-n't be happening. Not long ago this shutter at the front of the projec-tor fell down during the movie, blocking the light. Pff-ft! No picture. No way should that happen with a new projector." Rodney also tweaks movie film and moves objects around, both here and in the balcony projector booth. "He freaks people out sometimes," says McVay, who isn't worried about her cousin's ghost. "He was a real gentle guy. He loved animals, and he would never hurt a fly."

The side auditorium itself seems to be a favorite spot for the mean ghost in the past few years. McVay speculates that remodeling of the lobby and concession area in the mid-1990s may have brought the spirit out into the public areas. "We never used to sense him anywhere but backstage and on the third floor, but now he's seen not only in the lobby, but in both auditoriums on this floor." At least one patron has seen the specter in the lobby outside the side auditorium in the past 18 months, and a recent experience has left one member of the theatre staff reluctant to be in the auditorium alone. "Rozy was cleaning the auditorium after a show and saw the ghost standing next to the exit door on the right side of the theatre. He put down his broom and dustpan and came running out of the theatre," says McVay, chuckling. "Rozy is a great big tough-looking guy with dreadlocks. He's doesn't look like somebody who'd be afraid of ghosts, but he doesn't like to go in there anymore. When he went back to get his broom he was surprised to find that he hadn't just laid his stuff down. The broom and dustpan were probably 20 feet apart where he threw them."

Kara McVay is correct in thinking that the hidden parts of the Strand reveal how it could be haunted. The Strand Theatre has stood for nearly 90 years, and will probably stand for many more. It has been a busy existence, filled with comedy and drama that were not always confined to its stage or screens. Its contents, both beautiful and mundane, are the footprints of the thousands of lives that have crossed its thresholds, leaving traces of themselves in every corner. One might wonder instead how the Strand could possibly not be haunted, considering the many souls the old building has seen come and go.

Or not.

*Above, the presidential car that bore Lincoln's body back to Illinois;
below, Lincoln's funeral cortege in Columbus.*

Abe's Eternal Ride Home

At midnight in the dark of an April night,

the air along the Conrail tracks north of Worthington turns deathly cold. Clouds cover the light of the moon and a sight more chilling than the frigid air appears: the pilot engine of a train moves silently south as though on rails of velvet. Following the engine's ghostly lead, a train of eight dark, garlanded funeral cars glides by on wheels as quiet as the tomb. The final car, a deep chocolate brown color and bearing the coat of arms of the United States, carries the body of assassinated President Abraham Lincoln on its eternal journey back to Illinois.

The death of Abraham Lincoln only days after Robert E. Lee's surrender at Appomattox Court House shook the nation to its core. Having already endured four years of a bloody war to keep the Union intact, citizens now faced the prospect of reuniting and healing the deeply divided "United" States without the man who had guided them through the darkest days in U.S. history.

The funeral train bearing the remains of Lincoln and of his son Willie, who had died in 1862 and was to be reinterred beside his father in Illinois, left Washington at 8:00 a.m. on Friday, April 21, 1865. The train reversed most of the route by which Lincoln had arrived in Washington for his inauguration four years earlier, stopping in Baltimore; Harrisburg, Pennsylvania; Philadelphia; New York City; Albany; Westfield, New York; Cleveland; Columbus; Indianapolis; Michigan City, Indiana; Chicago and finally its destination, Springfield, Illinois. All along the route, thousands of mourners lined the tracks to pay their respects. In Baltimore, 10,000 people filed past the open coffin in three hours as it lay in state.

In Harrisburg, 40,000 lined the streets as the hearse carrying the President's remains wound through the city; in Philadelphia, police estimated 300,000 citizens passed by the coffin to pay their respects. Even in rural areas and small towns, hundreds and sometimes thousands of people stood by the tracks — many in the pouring rain that seemed to shadow the stately cortege — as the train slowly made its way across the country.

The citizens of Columbus draped the city's buildings in mourning for President Lincoln.

The procession pulled into Columbus's Union Station at 7:30 a.m. on Saturday, April 29, where it was met by a group of 14 honorary pallbearers. The coffin was placed on a 17-foot-long hearse drawn by white horses and taken to the rotunda of the Ohio Statehouse, where it was placed on a low, flower-covered dais for public viewing. An estimated 50,000 central Ohioans filed past before the remains were returned to the train station for departure to Indianapolis at 8:00 that evening to continue the journey to Springfield, where Lincoln and son Willie were laid to rest in the Lincoln tomb at Oak Ridge Cemetery.

Many who study paranormal phenomena believe that a haunting can result from a highly emotional event "imprinting" itself on a site, replaying the feelings and sights of the original event over and over—a psychic film loop. Perhaps it is no surprise, then, that in the nearly 140 years since the paroxysm of grief caused by Lincoln's death, the ghostly funeral train has made its yearly visit in locations all along the route of the earthly procession. It has been reported in upstate New York, near Albany; Pennsylvania; Delaware and Franklin counties in Ohio; Indiana; and Illinois. Always, it is near midnight. Always, there is an unearthly chill along the tracks. Always, the train is silent, gliding unheard along the tracks as it bears its precious cargo to the eternal quiet of the grave.

A Postscript: Lincoln and the Supernatural

Abraham Lincoln, American icon, is remembered as the man who won the Civil War, freed the slaves, refused to back down to the demands of pro-slavery factions—all of which are true, if over-simplified, accomplishments. Lincoln was a complex man, intelligent, sometimes conflicted in his views on slavery and equal rights, and given to periods of deep depression. He also believed in such para-normal phenomena as clairvoyance and precognition and, though not a Spiritualist, he participated in some of his wife Mary's attempts to contact the spirit of their son Willie, who died at the White House early in Lincoln's administration.

Lincoln had a number of experiences of precognition during his life, most famously predicting his own death in office—not once, but twice. In a vision that occurred before the end of his first term in office, he looked into a mirror and saw a double image of himself, one clear and one a ghostly double of his face. He interpreted the vision to mean that he would win re-election but would not live through his second term. Only a few days before his fatal encounter with John Wilkes Booth, Lincoln dreamed of a coffin in the White House; when he approached a guard to ask who was lying in state in the President's house, he was told, "The assassinated President." In the dream, he then approached the coffin and saw himself lying inside it. In his last Cabinet meeting before the fateful trip to Ford's Theatre, several of the secretaries were disturbed by the fatalistic cast of his comments, which seemed to indicate a belief that he would die soon.

Besides having several paranormal experiences during his life, Lincoln's spirit seems to have kept itself busy since his death. Mr. Lincoln has been seen finishing an interrupted waltz with Kate Chase at the Ohio Statehouse (see *Columbus Ghosts: Historical Haunts of Ohio's Capital*). Statehouse employees and visitors have also reported seeing his coffin in the rotunda there. And of course, Lincoln's specter has been seen or sensed many times in the White House by both occupants and guests including Theodore Roosevelt, Dwight Eisenhower, Harry Truman, Grace Coolidge, Queen Wilhelmina of the Netherlands and Eleanor Roosevelt, whose personal secretary ran screaming from the second floor after having seen Lincoln's apparition seated on the bed in the Lincoln Bedroom, pulling on his boots. Winston Churchill did not like to sleep in the Lincoln Bedroom and was often found to have moved across the hall during the night.

Lincoln was a man of deep and often melancholy feelings, aged prematurely by the responsibilities of his office during his country's lowest moments. Perhaps the pressure and turmoil of his life caused his soul to leave its imprint in many places, or perhaps Abe is still trying to complete the unfinished business of his life. Whatever the reason, and despite his foreknowledge of his own death, Abraham Lincoln is still frequently present in our present world.

The Hilltop home's blackened limestone sills may bear mute testimony to a tragic tale.

The Light Hurt My Children

The house sits quietly on a narrow brick street

in the Hilltop west of downtown Columbus. It is a large red brick home, built around the turn of the twentieth century. Tara Robinson* bought the house six years ago. Once a boarding house, it had been divided into seven apartments that included rooms in the attic and the basement. Robinson was well aware that she was buying a fixer-upper and that she and her boyfriend, Rob*, would be putting a lot of time and effort into the house. She wasn't expecting an unapprecia-tive audience for their renovations.

"The first time anything happened, I was upstairs in the hall strip-ping wallpaper and Rob was working on something downstairs," says Robinson. The upstairs hall is a square area. Facing the hall from the stairs, the door to Robinson's computer room is to the left. Opposite the stairway is the bathroom; on the right wall are the doors to Robinson's bedroom and another room used for exercise equipment. At a right angle to the exercise room door on the same wall as the staircase is the closed door to the attic stairs.

"I was working on the wall next to the computer room door and had my back to the open door to the exercise room," says Robinson, "when I had this strange — it's hard to describe — kind of a subliminal image in my mind. It was like I was working on the wall but I could also see behind me. I saw the silhouette of a woman standing in the doorway to the exercise room. She was fairly short, maybe five-foot-four, and had long hair pulled up on top of her head in a Gibson girl style. She was wearing a long dress with long sleeves and a high neckline like the ones where you wear a brooch at the neck. She seemed very sad — and she wondered what I was doing."

Shaken, Robinson went downstairs without turning to look at the doorway. "I kept thinking, 'Now, what movie have I seen that this came from?' I tried to rationalize it, and I didn't say anything to Rob about what had happened. I figured he'd think I was crazy."

Weeks passed without further visits from the mysterious woman. But other odd things began to happen. A battery-operated smoke detector in the hall outside the exercise room began to malfunction, going off at odd times. "It would go off as I was leaving for work," says Robinson. "I'd go out and lock the door and hear it going off inside. One day it did it three times. I'd go back in and find nothing wrong, fan around the smoke detector for a minute, and it would shut off. I'd go out and start to lock the door and it would go off again. After the third time I took it down and pulled the batteries out, thinking it was just a bad unit. But the new one I replaced it with did the same thing."

Robinson had a security system installed after she came to work on the house and discovered some neighborhood boys had broken in. The system was hardwired and designed to go off at the security company's office as well as at the house. Like the smoke alarm, the security system began to go off for no apparent reason. Stranger still, it rang only at the house, not at the security company's office — although if Robinson deliberately tripped it as a test, it rang at both places.

A battery-operated doorbell also joined in the electrical mayhem, ringing repeatedly when there was no one at the door.

"We didn't know *what* was going on," says Robinson. "We tried to blame the smoke detector and the doorbell on bad batteries, but then why would the security alarm do the same thing? It didn't *have* batteries."

After weeks of dealing with false alarms once or twice a week, it seemed to Robinson that the disturbances were most frequent between 2:30 and 4:30 in the morning. Once the smoke detector, the security alarm and the doorbell all went off simultaneously in the dead of night.

Then, about six months after her vision of the woman in the upstairs doorway, Robinson had another visitor.

Alone in the house, she was sitting at the dining room table reading a book for a class. Sitting with her back to the stairway, she suddenly became aware of a presence moving down the stairs. It was as though she was seeing the scene from some point above herself. "This time it was a man," she says. "He came down the stairs very quickly and stopped behind me, looking over my shoulder like he was trying to see what I was doing. He was wearing a suit with a vest and trousers, but no jacket. It was kind of a dark pinstripe pattern on a lighter background, but the whole thing was kind of monochromatic, so I couldn't tell what color. He had on a white shirt with the sleeves pulled or folded back so the cuffs were up near his shoulders. It felt like his head was right next to mine." Summoning her courage, Robinson turned her head toward the presence at her shoulder — and saw nothing.

Several weeks later, the man returned, this time standing behind Robinson on the stairs as she sanded the walls in the stairwell.

Robinson still had not said anything to her boyfriend, Rob, fearing his reaction. That changed one Sunday morning as the two left to go out for breakfast.

As they closed the front door, Robinson asked if Rob was going to turn off the TV he had left playing in the living room. After a moment's thought, he said "No, I think I'll leave it on for the ghosts."

Shocked, Robinson demanded to know what he was talking about. His reply chilled her: In the evenings while she was in classes,

Rob often sat in the living room watching TV — and listening to people walking around upstairs. "Again, I tried to rationalize it," says Robinson. "You know … maybe it was the cats. Maybe it was the neighbors he was hearing. Maybe it was the wind. But he was convinced that he was hearing footsteps."

Rob had also seen presences in the house, but differently from the mental images Robinson had seen. Sitting in the living room, Rob would sometimes see heads — no bodies — in his peripheral vision, passing through the area between the stairway and the kitchen. When he looked directly at the area, they would disappear, only to reappear in his peripheral vision as soon as he turned away.

Comparing experiences, Robinson and her boyfriend were convinced they had spirit presences in the house, but undecided about what they should do. The visitors had not been particularly threatening. Robinson had sensed great sadness from the woman, and both spirits seemed to be curious about what she was doing in the house. However, things changed with Robinson's fourth visit from beyond.

While working on a project in the living room, Robinson realized she had left the hammer lying upstairs in one of the bedrooms. Leaving Rob holding a heavy piece of wood in place downstairs, she ran up the steps to retrieve the hammer. As she ran back down the stairs, she suddenly became aware that the ghostly man was behind her, chasing her down the steps. "I got to the bottom step and kind of froze. I could sense him standing on the landing above me, and he was angry, shaking his fists at me. He didn't want me there."

Frightened, Robinson didn't turn around, but continued into the living room without looking back.

That Halloween Robinson hosted a costume party at the house, hiring a Tarot reader to entertain her guests. Unfortunately the reader had to cancel at the last minute, but gave her the phone number of someone else who might be able to help. That call led to Deb Hinty, a Columbus-area psychic who agreed to bring her Tarot cards to the party on short notice. The night of the party, Robinson led Hinty up to the computer room, where she had a table set up for her. Making small talk, Hinty complimented Robinson on the house, commenting that she had gotten it at a great price. Taken aback, Robinson was convinced at first that Hinty was a fake who had been checking real estate records to get information on her. Then Hinty revealed that she sensed five spirits in the house. Surprised, Robinson countered that there were only two, a man and a woman. Hinty agreed that the man and the woman were there, and described the woman fully. "Yes, that's her," stammered Robinson. "How did you know that?"

"Because she's standing right there next to you," replied Hinty gently, pointing to an area at Robinson's elbow.

Deb Hinty remembers Tara's house well. "I was setting up my table and I kept seeing this man in the doorway to the room I was in," says Hinty. "He was making motions like he was pounding on the door to the room, even though it was open, and appeared to be shouting or screaming. Then I realized there was a whole family of spirits in the house."

"Deb told me that the couple's three children were also in the house, and that she didn't know how I could not be aware of them because they were always around me, pulling on my clothes to get my attention," says Robinson. "And then I remembered an awful dream that I'd had some time before."

In the dream, Robinson was in the yard behind the house, facing toward the garage at the back corner of the lot. "I was wearing jeans and a loose shirt," Robinson says, "and something was pulling at the sides of my shirt. I couldn't see anything, but it was just like two little kids pulling in a different direction on each side. It felt like they were trying to pull me toward the garage. I looked back in the corner of the yard by the garage, and there was a really old-fashioned tricycle there, floating a few inches above the ground. The tricycle started to come toward me like someone was riding it. I wanted to get away but I couldn't move. The tricycle kept coming at me, and then, just before it got to me, I woke up."

Hinty asked if Robinson wanted to know what she sensed had happened in the house that left the ghostly family trapped there. Pointing toward the closed door of the exercise room, Hinty indicated correctly that there was a fireplace in that room — the only fireplace on the floor. "That room was the master bedroom," she said. When it was cold the whole family slept in there. One night an ember escaped the fireplace and started a fire. The woman died trying to get the children out. The man died trying to put out the fire." Then, chillingly: "The man doesn't want you here."

After hearing Hinty's story about her alleged ghosts, Robinson began researching the house. Unfortunately, turn-of-the-century records are scanty. The street is first listed in the 1894–95 Columbus city directory. The first listing found of an occupant at Robinson's address was in 1907, when Isaac Braithwaite occupied the home. However, Braithwaite and his wife had no young children; nor did any of the families following until around 1920. Since the spirits' clothing was clearly from the early years of the century, perhaps the tragedy occurred before the Braithwaites' occupancy of the house — or perhaps the street numbers were altered at some point and one of the other families listed on that street in the 1900 census were the victims. Fire department records for the early 1900s are also incomplete; ironically, many city records were lost in a fire at City Hall around 1910.

Robinson has not done any renovations to the exercise room that are extensive enough to have revealed any hidden fire damage, but she has noticed that some of the limestone trim on that corner of the house is blackened. "It looks like someone has tried to remove it with a wire brush, but you can still see it in places," she says.

And the ghost family? Robinson was undecided at first about whether to seek someone's help to remove her unwilling cohabitants. Then one night as she sat on her bed studying with both of her cats asleep beside her, the cats both awakened suddenly, staring at the empty doorway. She watched as they stared fixedly at the doorway for several minutes; then both their heads turned in unison as though watching something cross the room to the headboard behind Robinson. "I jumped up and yelled, 'Enough! This is my room and my house and I want you to get out of here right now!' and slammed the bedroom door." Then she called Deb Hinty.

A few days later Hinty arrived to cleanse the house. Also present was Brenda, a medium. As Brenda sat down in the living room, she announced, "She doesn't want to leave. She wants you to go."

Through Brenda, the spirit woman in the house argued that this was her house and she didn't want to leave. Hinty insisted that the family had to go, that they no longer belonged in the house, that they should move toward the light and move on from the place where they had been trapped for a hundred years. Finally, the crux of the matter was reached: Brenda said the woman did not want to go toward the light because "the light had hurt her children."

Hinty gently explained to the frightened spirit that the light was not the fire that had hurt her children, but a place that would release them all from the house where they had died. At last, they could rest.

After the cleansing, Robinson says the difference in the house's atmosphere was remarkable, especially in the upstairs hallway. "It always seemed like the air was really close, like it was actually hard to breathe in the corner outside the exercise room. After Deb came it was like someone had opened a window upstairs and let in fresh air. Before, I always unconsciously walked out around that corner when I went upstairs to my bedroom. Now I walk straight across it."

A few weeks after the cleansing, the doorbell rang one evening as Rob and Tara were watching TV. No one was there. "I called Deb Hinty and told her about it, but she said sometimes the spirits will come back briefly, almost as thought they're saying good-bye." It was the last unusual occurrence in the home.

The old apple trees on Davidson Road are the last witnesses to a sad Hilliard haunting.

Welcome to Haunted Hilliard

Hilliard Davidson High School is NOT what most people would picture as a "haunted schoolhouse." Opened in 1989, the school is open, bright and airy, with two stories of classrooms and a large common area on the first floor. Students bustle through the halls between classes, very much alive.

And yet, there ARE stories about uncanny happenings in the halls of Hilliard Davidson...

The Pipe-Smoking Teacher

Kim Shepherd has taught English in the Hilliard School system for more than 20 years. One of the first teachers assigned to the new high school, he taught English and creative writing across the hall from his friend Rob Burkhardt*, who taught American Literature. Although the two had never crossed paths there, both had graduated from The Ohio State University and remembered seeing each other on campus. As hip young intellectuals in the late sixties, both had experimented with smoking pipes. The two teachers had many shared interests and became good friends, often running or biking together.

In the summer of 1995, Rob Burkhardt took a trip to California. He had his bike with him, and was still running regularly—a healthy man, 47 years old, well-conditioned and energetic. However, as he fetched his bike to go riding on the morning of July 7, something went horribly wrong. Another man who was rooming with him saw him go for his bike, then heard a thud as Rob collapsed to the floor. An ambulance was called, but efforts to resuscitate him failed. Rob Burkhardt was dead.

The news came as a shock to his colleagues in Hilliard, sudden and totally unexpected. There was no warning, no time to adjust, no time to say good-bye. For schools, however, as with the theatre, the show must go on. That fall a new English teacher took Rob's place and life at Hilliard Davidson continued.

About four years after Rob Burkhardt's death, Kim Shepherd was in his classroom one day in late summer, preparing for the new school year. Across the hall in Rob's former classroom, Tracy Peters* was also making preparations for the new term. Peters and another teacher who had been talking in the hall and in Peters's classroom knocked on Shepherd's door to ask him a strange question: Had Rob Burkhardt smoked a pipe?

"Yeah, he did," said Shepherd curiously. "Why?"

Peters had noticed something very strange in her classroom. Shepherd says, "There was one spot, maybe two or three feet across, where there was a distinct odor of pipe tobacco. There were no windows open, and we were the only three people on the floor. There was no smell in the rest of the room—just that one little area."

The incident happened about four years after Rob died, says Shepherd. "I wondered—if it was really Rob—why it was so long before he came back."

Perhaps the habits of this life persist after death, and Rob Burkhardt was preparing for his new school year on the Other Side. Or maybe he just wanted to say a long-delayed goodbye.

Fergus Takes a Bow

Theatre ghosts are a very old tradition. It's hard to find a theatre of any age without at least one phantom actor or actress or dedicated patron who continues to hang around in spirit form, causing varying degrees of mischief.

The auditorium at Hilliard Davidson seems young to have yet acquired its own theatre ghost, but many students tell the story of Fergus, who is said to haunt the stage area.

The story of Fergus begins in the early 1800s, when the land where Hilliard Davidson sits was owned by a well-to-do farmer. In those days, it was common to pass land to the oldest son, who was expected to stay there and farm as his father had done. Fergus was the farmer's oldest son — but he had no desire to farm the father's land some day. Fergus wanted to act. As the son of a wealthy man, he had perhaps seen more of the world than the typical Ohio farm boy. Not for Fergus the plows and harrows of the farm; he wished for the lime-light and the drama of the stage.

Unable to reconcile himself to the future expected by his family, Fergus ran away to New York. His father, equally determined to make Fergus toe his line, sent Pinkerton detectives after him. Returned to Ohio against his will, Fergus was kept under virtual house arrest by his father.

Still unable to face life as a farmer, Fergus took his own life — at least that of his physical body. But those who spend time onstage at Hilliard Davidson think that Fergus, denied the New York stage during his life, has taken up residence with the theatre program that sits on the land he would have inherited. He makes himself known in movements on the catwalks over the stage, knocking down dust and small debris from areas where no visible person walks. Sometimes he shows up in unexplained disturbances in sound equipment — faint voices heard on headphones or crackling static with no apparent cause. And occasionally he walks across the stage he aspired to grace, his footsteps sounding where no one can be seen.

Haunted Farmhouse

The white farmhouse still stood in 1997. On Davidson Road across from the dead end of Heather Ridge Drive, it stood alone and boarded up, an ancient pole with the remains of a basketball hoop, a wooden mailbox bearing the name "Windmiller" and a group of apple trees to its east the last reminders that families once lived there and children once played in its yard. It was torn down sometime around the end of 1999; only the apple trees, which still bear fruit each fall, still stand.

Kim Shepherd's creative writing classes complete a unit on folklore and urban legends each year, during which students are encouraged to share their own tales and ghost stories. One year a student shared a tale about the white farmhouse.

The student's father had briefly lived in the old house as a boy. He and his brother shared a room on the second floor, below the house's small attic. One night, the two boys had gone to bed when they heard noises in the unused attic, as though someone were moving around in the empty space. Frightened, the boys ran into their parents' room. Assuring the boys that it was probably squirrels, or maybe just the wind, the parents allowed the boys to sleep with them that night.

The second time the boys heard the noises, the parents were less sympathetic. This time the father returned to the room with the boys, but there were no noises to be heard while he was there. With more assurances that they were hearing animal noises or their imaginations, the boys were tucked back in.

The third time the frightened boys heard the noises, their father told them that the next day he would prove to them that there was nothing there to be afraid of. The following morning, the father and the two boys climbed into the attic with a bag of flour, which they sprinkled about on the floor. The father was certain that if the noises came again, they would find squirrel or raccoon footprints in the flour, proving that the boys were being carried away by their imaginations.

Now the boys were as excited that they would actually find out what was in the attic as their father was certain that he already knew. The next time the sounds came from the attic, the father and the two boys climbed into the attic again. They did indeed find footprints in the flour — small *human* footprints.

Mary Weaver Miller graduated from Hilliard High School in 1932 and lived in the city all her life. She was a founder of the Northwest Franklin County Historical Society and kept her own journals filled with stories and news from the Hilliard area. The father with the mysterious footsteps in his attic once talked to Mrs. Miller about the house, wondering if she knew of any odd stories about the place.

She did, and was surprised he hadn't heard them too. About 20 years before the puzzled father and his family had moved into the house, a family with a chronically ill daughter had lived there. Although the local doctors tried, they were unable to do much for the girl, who eventually died in the house. Following her death, several families had lived in the house — but none had stayed long. It seemed that the young girl who had died there had left in body only.

And why did only the boys hear the noises of the little ghost in the attic? After all those years alone, maybe she just wanted to play.

Dr. James Howard Snook, ca. 1930.

The Murderous Dr. Snook

He had it all: a successful academic career, the respect of his colleagues, a devoted wife, a beautiful child, even an Olympic medal. Why, then, did James Howard Snook's life end with a secret dawn burial in an unmarked grave? Why, even after more than 70 years, is the location of his grave at Green Lawn Cemetery unrevealed for fear of vandalism? And why is his unquiet shade still sometimes seen walking the cemetery where his mortal remains lie?

Snook's scandalous fall from grace shook Columbus in 1929, focusing national attention on a story so lurid that its sordid details were carefully edited out of the "complete" transcripts of his trial that were published in the Columbus newspapers. Persons under the age of 18 were banned from the courtroom, where curious onlookers filled the public seats, often arriving at 3 a.m. to wait for the courtroom doors to open at nine o'clock.

James Snook met Theora Kathleen Hix in June of 1926. He was 46, a horse surgeon and professor of pharmacology at the Ohio State College of Veterinary Medicine, married to the former Helen Marple.

Hix was 21, an Ohio State medical student who planned to spend the summer working as a relief operator on the University Hospital switchboard and as a university stenographer. Snook offered Hix a ride back to her room at Mack Hall one rainy evening. Less than a month later the two were lovers.

The pair met two or three times a week at varying locations around the city, or sometimes drove into the country in Dr. Snook's dark blue Ford coupe. After Hix was frightened by an attempted break-in at her Mack Hall room, Snook, a member of the U.S. pistol-shooting team that had won a gold medal at the 1920 Olympic games in Antwerp, gave her a Remington derringer to protect herself. The two sometimes practiced shooting at the New York Central shooting range on Fisher Road near McKinley Avenue. By 1929, Snook had rented a room on Hubbard Avenue — in his real name — to use as a trysting place, representing himself as a traveling salt salesman who used the room to meet with his "wife" when she could come into town. The landlady suspected nothing, later testifying that she remembered Hix as very quiet and looking like a "country woman."

Despite their frequent meetings and lack of concern about hiding their identities, the pair apparently managed to keep their liaison a secret. Although rumors circulated among the staff at the College of Veterinary Medicine that Dr. Snook was a womanizer, no one had a clue as to the identity of his possible female companions. Hix was likewise discreet; her roommates later described her as a studious girl who seldom had dates, didn't discuss any male friends, and liked to take long walks alone, often late at night.

What drove James Snook and Theora Hix? Snook was a quiet, taci-turn man with few friends. He had recently shown signs of restlessness and a certain boredom with his work. Although his wife later staunchly declared him to be a kind, considerate man and their mar-riage a happy one, she also admitted in 1929 that she felt that she had lost him, little by little, over the previous few years.

Hix was intelligent and independent, and despite her later portrayal as the unfortunate victim of an older man, was no innocent lamb. Snook was not her first lover. She frankly admitted during their affair that she was intimately involved with another man and was not above making unflattering comparisons between Snook and her younger paramour. Hix was demanding and could be cruel. She also experimented freely with aphrodisiacs and other drugs, some of which Snook acquired for her and tried himself.

Whatever their differences, the physical attraction between the pair fueled their relationship for three years. Then, on June 13, 1929, the affair ended, suddenly and horribly.

On Friday afternoon, June 14, two 16-year-old boys at the New York Central shooting range found a woman's battered body lying in the weeds. The same afternoon, Hix's roommates, Beatrice and Alice Bustin, filed a missing persons report after Hix failed to return to their Neil Avenue rooms on Thursday night or Friday morning. The Bustins were called to the Glenn L. Myers mortuary on Second Avenue, where they identified the body from the shooting range as Theora Hix.

Hix's death had been violent and gruesome. Dr. Joseph Murphy, the Franklin County Coroner, found several deep blows to her head that appeared to have been inflicted with a ball peen hammer. At least one of the blows broke her skull and drove bone fragments into her brain. The actual cause of death, however, was the severing of the jugular vein and carotid artery on the left side of her neck, carried out with a skill suggesting a killer with a thorough knowledge of anatomy.

Combing the shooting range for clues, the police found a broken key ring that included the key to the Hubbard Avenue love nest, where the landlady identified Snook as the man who rented the room. He was quickly arrested. Also arrested was Marion T. Meyers of the Ohio State agriculture department and the Franklin County Extension service — Hix's former lover, who had drawn attention to himself by calling the funeral home after learning of Hix's death. Meyers was quickly exonerated. After intense around-the-clock grilling by the police, Snook dictated and signed a confession on June 20, a week after Hix's murder.

Snook's guilt was difficult to dispute. Bloodstains matching Hix's blood type were found in his car; he was in possession of a ball peen hammer which also bore telltale blood spots, as did the clothing he had worn the night of the murder. And as a veterinary surgeon, he certainly possessed the skill needed to neatly sever the large vein and artery in Hix's neck.

The trial lasted less than a month. Witnesses included Snook's wife Helen, who maintained that her husband was an even-tempered and peaceful man, never abusive or quarrelsome. She declared in court, "He couldn't have hurt anybody — no, not anything, of his own accord. Always so kind — so thoughtful — so considerate — so generous. How could I forget that?" Snook's mother also testified to her son's consideration and good character. When James Snook himself took the stand, both women left the courtroom.

Snook's story, told with a chilling calmness, was that of a man in over his head, who found himself and his family threatened by a jealous, possessive Theora Hix. The afternoon of the murder, he said, he had driven to the Scioto Country Club for a round of golf. At the fifth hole, he was interrupted by Theora Hix, who walked onto the course and asked him to leave with her. Not wanting to leave his companions in the middle of the game, he asked her to wait until he reached the ninth hole, when he could more politely bow out of the foursome. Hix was insistent. "You have to help me out," she said repeatedly. Not wishing for any more of a scene, Snook complied and walked back to the clubhouse to bathe and change clothes.

The two drove the Ford coupe to the New York Central shooting range, parking in a secluded area where they could be intimate without drawing attention. After a time, Snook told her he had to leave, as he was going to visit his mother that weekend and needed to go home and prepare for the trip. Hix became angry, demanding that he stay in Columbus with her. The argument escalated, and Hix threatened harm to Snook's mother, his wife, and his two-year old-daughter. "Damn the baby!" Hix screamed. "I'll kill her, too!" Then, according to Snook's testimony, she violently attacked him, biting him several times as he attempted to push her away. Hix climbed out of the car, turned her back and began digging in her purse. Fearing she was looking for her gun, Snook hit her in the head with a ball peen hammer he kept in the car. As Hix staggered away, Snook followed her, falling out of the car. He hit her several more times — he couldn't remember how many — then found himself sitting on the running board alone. Hix, who was lying in the weeds a few feet from the car, was silent, though he claimed to have called to her several times.

Snook's story varied somewhat on the subject of cutting Hix's neck. At first he claimed not to remember doing so, but then stated he had cut her throat "because I didn't want to see her suffer."

Snook drove away in the Ford, taking the hammer and recovering Hix's purse from the weeds. On the way home he threw the purse out the window along the side of the road. He did not go to his mother's that weekend, but spent some time cleaning the blood from his car and the hammer — not thoroughly enough, it turned out. The blood-spots on both were damning evidence when he was arrested two days later.

When the case was sent to the jury on August 14, 1929, it took a mere 28 minutes to return a verdict: guilty of murder in the first degree. Mercy was not recommended. Snook was executed by electrocution at the Ohio Penitentiary on February 28, 1930. His body was taken to his home on Tenth Avenue, where a small private service was held at 5 a.m. on March 1, followed by immediate burial at Green Lawn.

Helen Snook stood by her husband until the end, visiting him often. She shared his last meal and was with him in his cell until shortly before he was taken to the execution chamber. Snook told the press that he had never really appreciated his wife until it was too late.

Perhaps the self-possessed Dr. Snook really had come to appreciate his loyal spouse, but a more telling measure of the man was revealed in the *Columbus Evening Dispatch* on the evening of Dr. Snook's burial under the headline, "Killing of Miss Hix Was Premeditated, Snook Tells Warden." In a conversation with penitentiary warden Preston Thomas shortly before the execution, Snook revealed that Hix's murder was planned, not committed in the heat of their argument. In this final confession, Snook claimed to have carried the hammer and knife with him so that he had weapons close at hand. The demand by Hix to drive to the shooting range had provided Snook with his first opportunity to carry out the killing, which he tried to make appear the work of "a maniac." Snook regretted his fabricated story only because he thought that it had hurt his case with the jury. He described the killing as the "logical and inevitable conclusion to [a] 'convenient arrangement.'"

Dr. Snook's "convenient arrangement" cost more than the life of Theora Hix; it cost Helen Snook and her daughter their husband and father, Snook's mother her only son and Theora Hix's elderly parents their dearly-loved daughter. It blackened the name of James Howard Snook forever. Perhaps the lonely soul in the natty gray suit, crisp hat and distinctive nose glasses who is seen walking among the stones at Green Lawn Cemetery is doomed to walk there until he has fully atoned for the damage. Perhaps eternity is too short a time.

Does Hiram Perkins' spirit still look to the heavens?

Hiram's Eternal Dream

Pigs, the Union Army and a frugal math professor.
An unlikely trio, but one that led to the construction of one of
Delaware County's most distinctive landmarks — and one of central
Ohio's most enduring ghost stories.

Hiram Perkins was a professor of Mathematics and Astronomy at
Ohio Wesleyan University when the Civil War broke out in 1861.
A dutiful man, he promptly left his teaching position intending to
join the Union Army. Unfortunately his patriotic intentions were
thwarted when the 6'1", 97-pound professor was rejected as unfit for
service. Still determined to aid the Union cause, Perkins returned to
his family's pig farm in southern Ohio and spent the war raising hogs
to provide food for Union soldiers.

Then, as now, defense contracting could be a very lucrative business, and Perkins' hogs brought a great deal of money from the gov-
ernment. However, as a devout Methodist he felt it would be immoral
for him to personally benefit from the sufferings of the war, so he
invested the money and returned to his teaching duties after the war
ended, living off his modest salary, never more than $1,200 per year.

Perkins retired from Ohio Wesleyan in 1907, and began working on a project dear to his heart: an observatory to be built in central Ohio. He began with modest goals, but quickly realized that the return on his investments and his careful savings through the years would allow him to build a world-class facility. After working on his plans for 15 years, he finally saw ground broken for his dream in 1923 at the age of 90. Sadly, he did not live to see his observatory completed; he died about halfway through the building's construction, after his family brought him to the site and propped him up so that he could see the progress on his lifelong dream one last time.

Perkins Observatory opened in 1924 using a 60-inch telescope mirror borrowed from Harvard University. In 1931 a 69-inch mirror was completed and installed, the third largest in the world at that time. The observatory also housed one of the the best astronomical libraries of the day and facilities for visiting astronomers. Hiram Perkins' dream was a jewel set in the green fields of central Ohio, a demonstration of what one man's spirit can accomplish in life — and return to in death. For over the years, the scientists and students from Ohio Wesleyan and Ohio State who have used the observatory have reported many mysterious noises in the dark hours of the night. Tappings. Squeakings and creakings and groanings without any apparent source. They say that it's Hiram Perkins' ghost, come back to enjoy his creation, or perhaps to explore the skies again from a human perspective.

Tom Burns, the director of Perkins Observatory, says with a smile, "Of course, we don't believe in ghosts here — we're all a bunch of technical geeks. But we do believe in spirits, and Hiram Perkins' spirit is in everything here." On the other hand, says Burns, "The observatory dome acts like a sound board in here when it's quiet. When you're in here at 3 a.m. without much sleep, the sounds are — well, you start thinking it's time to go home."

And time for the gentle ghost of Hiram Perkins to gaze into infinity... for all of eternity.

A Postscript: Hiram's Mirror

If Hiram Perkins' ghost does indeed walk in Perkins Observatory, he has seen many changes over the years. One wonders what he would have to say about his wandering telescope mirror...

The 69-inch mirror was not only the third-largest telescope mirror in the world in 1931, it was also the first large mirror cast in the Western hemisphere. Performed by the U.S. Bureau of Weights and Measures, the casting process failed four times before the fifth blank was successfully cooled slowly enough to avoid distortions in the glass. Then an additional three years was needed to grind and polish the mirror. The finished mirror was 69 inches in diameter, 9.5 inches thick, and weighed 3,800 pounds — nearly two tons.

The mirror was used at Perkins Observatory for 30 years. However, conditions in central Ohio are not really conducive to telescope research; low elevations, cloudy weather conditions, humidity and the growth of Columbus and its attendant light and air pollution limited the usefulness of the huge mirror.

In 1961, the Perkins Telescope was moved to Lowell Observatory in Flagstaff, Arizona, where darker skies and better elevation and weather allowed for better data collection. It was the largest telescope ever moved. The 69-inch mirror stayed in Arizona for only a short while, however. It was soon replaced with a new 72-inch Pyrex mirror, a material much superior to the crown glass of the original.

And what does one do with a surplus 69-inch, two-ton glass mirror? In this case, the mirror returned to very near where it started. The mirror, still owned by Ohio Wesleyan University, was loaned to the Center of Science and Industry (COSI), which opened in Columbus in 1964. It was part of an optics display on the second floor for many years; when the display was changed, rather than try to move the mirror, a storage closet was built around it.

When COSI built a new facility in 2000, the mirror completed its long journey, returning at last to its original home at Perkins Observatory, where it is now on display.

Who is the beautiful lady heard sobbing in the woods of Delaware County?

The Pirate of Delaware County

Ohio in the early nineteenth century was wild and rough, still mostly covered with heavy forests. Only a few scattered communities of white settlers dotted the landscape. It was not a place where one would expect to find a stone castle, a volatile and mysterious artist, or a beautiful Spanish woman dressed in stiff brocades. Yet one of central Ohio's best-known ghost tales features all of these and more.

In 1833, the Scioto River Valley in southern Delaware County was a wonderland of oak, hickory, maple, walnut and sycamore trees standing untouched by human hands. In places the river banks rose in tall limestone cliffs 20 to 30 feet tall, overlooking the sparkling water flowing through the green valley below.

When the mysterious John Robinson arrived in Delaware that year, he stayed only briefly, heading out into the forest with his noticeably heavy packs. Finding a large tract of land along the river that suited him, Robinson paid for it in cash—by some accounts, in gold. He immediately hired workmen to erect a large stone house on the land, ordering the best materials for his new home and for the crypt he also built in the forest.

Naturally, the good citizens of Delaware County were agog at this apparently wealthy but reticent man. Who was he? Rumor had it that he was the somehow-disgraced son of an English nobleman, exiled to the New World to avoid a scandal back home. Reports of the fine fabrics and furnishings filling the stone "castle" flew around the county; the workmen spoke of the beautiful carved woodwork that Robinson himself was creating to ornament his new residence. The expected housewarming was eagerly awaited. What a sight the interior must be!

At last the construction was finished. Again, Robinson paid off the workmen in cash. No wonder those packs were so heavy, whispered the rumors. They must have been filled with gold!

However, the invitations to see the fabulous house never materialized. Instead, Robinson locked himself away in the forest, seen only rarely when shipments of artists' supplies were delivered to his door.

Angry at Robinson's unneighborly attitude, the local citizens were also consumed with curiosity about the mystery man. What was he *doing* out there alone?

The occasional workmen hired to make repairs at the castle brought back strange stories of fabulous paintings stacked throughout the house, produced by Robinson himself. The whispers centered around a particular painting of the rolling deck of a pirate ship in a storm at sea. The workmen who saw the painting swore that the face of the fierce pirate captain was the face of John Robinson himself!

While the townspeople of Delaware speculated about the source of John Robinson's gold, another mystery presented itself in the woods along the Scioto. A beautiful woman with black hair and eyes and creamy pale olive complexion was seen near the castle, walking along the riverbank or sitting on the rocks above the river. Her exotic coloring and the rich brocades she wore no doubt fueled rumors that she was a Spanish princess captured by the dread pirate captain, John Robinson, and held prisoner in his home. Those who saw the woman never heard her utter a sound, but late-night passers-by reported a woman's shrill cries and blood-curdling screams coming from the castle — the sounds of a woman being violently beaten.

Caught between fear of Robinson, curiosity, and the desire to rescue the unfortunate woman from her tormentor, local citizens hesitated to intervene at the great house. Finally, however, concern for the woman won out and a delegation of men approached the castle door. There was no answer to their knock. Carefully pushing the door open, they were met by a shocking sight: the house was deserted, apparently after a tremendous struggle had taken place there. Robinson's paintings lay about, slashed and torn. The worst was the library, where furniture was overturned and a dark liquid had been splashed and spattered on the walls and carpets. On the wall hung an incredibly beautiful full-length portrait of the woman wearing her fabulous brocades, eyes shining, lips parted just slightly. On the wall under the portrait was a single, tiny bloody handprint — the last trace of the portrait's subject.

Horrified, the men stared at the painting as it seemed to draw the breath of life. The luminous eyes filled with tears and the lips trembled as though about to speak. The terrified men bolted from the house without waiting to see what happened next.

The great castle stood deserted in the woods for some time before greed and curiosity overcame fear. Local folks began scavenging the rich carvings and furnishings from the house; others broke holes in the walls and dug around the house and on the grounds looking for the rest of John Robinson's pirate gold. Eventually the structure crumbled, its rubble covered by undergrowth. Only the unused crypt remained — and the stories told by those who passed by the site. They told of a beautiful woman seen in the woods by the river. Richly dressed, she walked through the trees on the bank and disappeared without a sound. Others who had reason to pass by at night heard the sobs and screams of a woman, carried on the wind through the trees — the desolate, eternal cries of the Spanish princess who vanished from the Delaware County woods as mysteriously as she had come.

Who Was John Robinson?

Yes, there was a real John Robinson. Unfortunately for the wonderful ghost story in which he stars, his life, while certainly colorful, wasn't nearly as romantic and mysterious as the story.

Though of French Huguenot ancestry, John Robinson was born in London, England, on March 21, 1802. A painter and sculptor, Robinson succeeded his father in the position of chief decorator of the Parliament Building and Windsor Castle. He married Elizabeth Hays in 1831. Shortly thereafter—sources place the date between 1832 and 1835—they emigrated to the U.S. after suffering a large loss in a fire. John Robinson was listed in a census of male inhabitants of Concord Township in Delaware County in 1835. According to one source, Robinson's wife died soon after coming to Delaware County and he married a local girl, the niece of Benajmin Hills, who lived near Robinson.

Robinson did indeed build a beautiful stone house that was the wonder of the area. It was said to be somewhat modeled after the style of an English baronial castle and beautifully furnished. While Robinson was not unfriendly with his neighbors, he was somewhat reclusive, preferring books and walks in the woods to conversations with the locals. It was scarcely the life of a hermit, however: he and his wife had six sons and a daughter. Robinson's castle burned in 1847, but he rebuilt it and continued to live there until 1853, when he moved to a 200-acre farm near Ostrander. There, he farmed and continued his painting and woodcarving. His carving work was well-known and featured in many local buildings, including the old Neil House Hotel in Columbus. After his wife's death in 1879, he made for himself a beautiful black walnut coffin with an ornately carved lid, which he stored in a hallway alcove until the time came to join her.

In 1891 Robinson was interviewed for the book *Portrait Gallery of Prominent Persons of Delaware County, Ohio with Biographical Narratives*. At the time, he was living on the Ostrander farm with his youngest son, Guido; all his children except his second son Alfred were still living. The book's authors described some of his paintings: a portrait of Chief Logan; an Italian landscape and castle, hanging over a carved mantelpiece; a vivid portrayal of a thunderstorm with a witch on a broomstick among the clouds representing "a besom of destruction."

As early as 1880, the "haunted castle" was well-known in Delaware County, even though the presumed villain of its story was still living quietly only a few miles from the site of the deserted house. What inspired the tale? Perhaps the sight of the beautiful home standing empty and crumbling in the woods and the unusual and romantic background of its former resident, stirred by years of rumors, were the real sources of the pirate story.

But who is to say that the soul of the real John Robinson doesn't occasionally visit the site of his beautiful home? Perhaps, late on a dark night a fortunate visitor would see, not a Spanish princess, but a white-haired, bearded man strolling the riverbank, admiring the long-gone maples and oaks. Perhaps.

Edward Orton's funeral cortege — but perhaps not his final appearance on the Ohio State University campus.

Five Little Ghosties

Among the grand historical ghosts and homes filled with spirits from cellar to rafters, there are the little ghost stories—quiet spirits, often anonymous, who go about their otherworldly business in homes, neighborhoods, businesses and cemeteries without fanfare. Here are a few little ghost stories from around central Ohio.

The Real Thurber Ghost

Fred Shannon, retired photographer for the *Columbus Dispatch*, photographed James Thurber many times during his career. After Thurber's death in 1961, Shannon attended an homage to the author at the Ohio State University, Thurber's Alma Mater.

The event was held in a room in the William Oxley Thompson Memorial Library on campus. There were several speakers in a panel setting, surrounded by framed Thurber cartoon art. A couple of hours into the event, in the middle of the discussion, one of Thurber's cartoons suddenly crashed to the floor, startling the speaker.

The cartoon had been hanging undisturbed for several hours. No one was near it when it fell, and the nail and picture wire appeared to be undamaged. Strange coincidence? Shannon doesn't think so.

"There was no reason for it to fall," says Shannon. His theory is that the subject of the homage decided to pay a little visit and stir things up a bit. "Thurber was kind of an ornery guy, you know. And that just looked like something he'd pull if he could."

Madame Sally

Sally Brunner and her husband Anton lived in a stately house on four acres situated along Alum Creek. The two apparently did well for themselves — the house cost $34,000 to build — although Anton's occupation was listed as "tinner" in the 1903–1907 Columbus city directory. Perhaps the fact that Sally ran a saloon out of the house explained their generous income. Or maybe it was the notorious bordello on South Grant Avenue, also run by Sally.

Sally and Anton's stay in their mansion was short. The saloon was forced out of business after complaints about the crowds and the rowdiness of its patrons, and in 1909 the house became a private residence of the Wilcox and Peters families, who held the mortgage. Later the house became the first home of the Columbus Academy, founded in 1911.

And the bordello? It, too, is long gone. But some fine evenings you might be lucky enough to spot an elegant woman, finely dressed in clothes from another age, strolling down the sidewalk near Grant and Town streets: Sally Brunner, taking care of business from the Other Side.

Swamp Road Sally

Swamp Road lies in Licking County, outside of Pataskala. It's a very rural area with few houses, mostly farm fields — and a long-time resident ghost.

"No one knows where she came from," says Matt Androsky. "I saw her out there one night around 12:00. We were driving down the road and saw her from maybe a quarter of a mile away. She was dressed in white, like a white dress or a nightgown, and she crossed the road in front of us, from right to left, then disappeared. This was September, and the fields on both sides of the road were bare, so there was nowhere for someone to hide. She was there, and then she was just gone."

Androsky is not the only one to have seen the phantom girl. Others have been startled to see a girl or young teenager crossing the road there late at night. One man thought he was about to hit the girl, and locking up his brakes in an effort to stop, swerved and totalled his truck.

They call her Swamp Road Sally. Was she a victim of an accident on the road? Did she live or die nearby? No one seems to know. We can only hope that someday she'll find what she's trying to reach on the other side of Swamp Road.

The Orton Hall Ghosts

The distinctive bell tower of Orton Hall rises above the south side of the Oval at the Ohio State University. The building's outer walls are of native Ohio stone, appropriate for the home of the Department of Geological Sciences, the Orton Memorial Library of Geology and the Orton Geological Museum. Rumor has it that there are also two less obvious inhabitants of the hall.

Edward Orton, the first president of Ohio State, loved the place and encouraged students to behave with appropriate decorum on its campus. Students claim that a light sometimes still flickers in the tower room where Dr. Orton used to read, and that those whose behavior in the building is found wanting are sometimes startled to encounter a sharp chill in the building—Dr. Orton's pointed warning to shape up.

The other spirit inhabitant of the hall is more unusual, described as a prehistoric man with thick, rough hair, a prominent forehead and a humped back, who can't speak but grunts and pounds on things (some wags have suggested that he is the spirit of a former football player). Dale Gnidevic, director of the museum, has encountered neither ghost. "They tell me they're here, but I've never seen them," he says.

Drop by Orton Hall sometime and check out the museum's displays. Maybe you'll get lucky and also spot a fellow visitor from another plane—and time.

Sources

Tina's Angry Spirit

Columbus Citizen Journal, various articles, April 9, 1984–April 14, 1984; "Group rules strange happenings were prompted by Tina, not 'force'," November 12, 1984.

Columbus Dispatch, various articles by Mike Harden and others, March 6, 1984–April 13, 1984; "The house is just a home—again," September 10, 1984; "Magician waves away paranormal," November 17, 1985; "Tina Resch: Hoopla fades, but questions linger," March 23, 1986.

Lubrano, Alfred, "In search of poltergeists." *Columbus Monthly*, April, 1984, pp. 101–104.

Phone interview with Fred Shannon, retired *Columbus Dispatch* photographer, December 2, 2002.

Phone interview with Mike Harden, *Columbus Dispatch* columnist, December 2, 2002.

Through a Glass, Darkly

Personal interview with Susan Hudak, December 5, 2002.

The Ghostly Piano Player

Borden, Jeff, "Little Theatre Group Says It Won't Abandon Season." *Columbus Dispatch*, October 13, 1978.

Borden, Jeff, "Official Narrowly Escapes as 'Little Theatre' Burns." *Columbus Dispatch*, October 12, 1978.

Personal interview and tour of Little Theatre Off Broadway with Jane Mixer and Joy Schmitt, November 14, 2002.

Wisehart, Sara, "Grove Cityans Proud of Theatre." *Columbus Dispatch*, February 1, 1970.

We're Here. They're Here.

Personal interview with Leigh Sutherly*, January 14, 2003.

The Ghostly Captain Dukeman

"Capt. George Dukeman Dies; City Fireman for 52 Years." *Columbus Citizen*, April 17, 1939.

"George Dukeman, City Fire Captain, Is Taken by Death." *Columbus Dispatch*,

April 17, 1939.

Personal interview and tour of Central Ohio Fire Museum with William T. Hall, Columbus Division of Fire Historian, December 5, 2002.

The Haunting of the Strand

Personal interview and tour of the Strand Theatre with Kara McVay, Chief Operating Officer, January 14, 2003.

Abe's Eternal Ride Home

http://members.aol.com/RVSNorton/Lincoln41.html, January 6, 2003.

http://members.aol.com/RVSNorton/Lincoln46.html, January 6, 2003.

http://members.aol.com/RVSNorton/Lincoln51.html, January 6, 2003.

Alexander, John. *Ghosts: Washington's Most Famous Ghost Stories.* 1988, The Washington Book Trading Company, Arlington, VA.

Borreson, Ralph. *When Lincoln Died.* ©1965 by Ralph Borreson, Appleton-Century, New York.

Donald, David Herbert, *Lincoln.* ©1995 by David Herbert Donald, Touchstone, New York.

Roberts, Nancy. *Civil War Ghosts and Legends.* 1992 by University of South Carolina. Metrobooks.

Switzer, John. "Time may be right for ghost train," *Columbus Dispatch,* Thursday, April 6, 1995.

The Light Hurt My Children

Personal interview with Deb Hinty, March 15, 2003.

Personal interview and tour of house with Tara Robinson*, February 2, 2003.

Polk's City Directory: Columbus, 1894 through 1920 editions.

U.S. Census Records, 1900, 1910, 1920, 1930.

Welcome to Haunted Hilliard

Personal interview with Kim Shepherd, December 12, 2002.

The Murderous Dr. Snook

http://www.shortnorth.com/Snook.html, January 31, 2003. Nancy Patzer, "The Trial of Dr. James Howard Snook."

http://www.vet.ohio-state.edc/docs/alpha/snook.htm, January 31, 2003.

Columbus Evening Dispatch and *Columbus Sunday Dispatch,* various articles, June 15–August 14, 1929; March 1, 1930

Columbus Citizen, various articles, March 1, 1930.

Lore, David. "The names of James Snook and Theora Hix are forever entwined in a sensational and tragic chapter in Ohio State history." *Ohio State Alumni Magazine,* November 1996, 22–28.

The Murder of Theora Hix: Dr. Snook's Uncensored Testimony (Trial held in Franklin County Court House, Columbus, Ohio August 1929). Published by Julius Diehr, 1929.

Hiram's Eternal Dream

http://www.perkins-observatory.org, March 18, 2003.
Phone interview with Tom Burns, director of Perkins Observatory, March 18, 2003.

The Pirate of Delaware County

http://www.forgottenoh.com
Helwig, Richard M., ed. *Ohio Ghost Towns #43 Delaware County.* Galena, Ohio: The Center for Ghost Town Research in Ohio.
History of Delaware County and Ohio. 1880, Chicago: O.L. Baskin & Co., Historical Publishers.
List of male inhabitants over the age of 21 living in Delaware County in year—1835. ©1988, George R. and Marilyn M. Cryder for Delaware County Chapter, OGS and Delaware County Historical Society. Inc.
Lytle, James R., ed. *20th Century History of Delaware County, Ohio and Representative Citizens.* 1908, Chicago: Biographical Publishing Company.
Portrait Gallery of Prominent Persons of Delaware County, Ohio, with Biographical Narratives. 1891, Mansfield, Ohio: The Biographical Publishing Company.
Woodyard, Chris. *Haunted Ohio III: Still More Ghostly Tales from the Buckeye State.* Kestrel Publications, Dayton, OH, 1994. Second printing, October 1995.

Five Little Ghosties

The Real Thurber Ghost
Phone interview with Fred Shannon, retired *Columbus Dispatch* photographer, December 2, 2002.

Madame Sally
Correspondence with Charles Miller, February 18, 2003 and March 19, 2003.

The Pataskala Ghost
Phone interview with Matt Androsky, March 25, 2003.

The Orton Hall Ghosts
http://www.forgottenoh.com
http://www.geology.ohio-state.edu/modules.php?op=modload&name= Dept_Info&file=Facilities
http://www.osu.edu/tour/tour6.html
Woodyard, Chris. *Haunted Ohio IV: Restless Spirits.* Kestrel Publications, Dayton, OH, 1997.

Haunted Sites You Can Visit

Information was current at the time this book was published, but it is always a good idea to call ahead in case schedules have changed.

Little Theatre Off Broadway
3981 Broadway
Grove City, OH 43123
614-875-3919 • www.ltob.org
Call for more information, upcoming plays and ticket prices.

Central Ohio Fire Museum
260 N. Fourth St. (intersection of Fourth and Chestnut streets)
Columbus, OH 43215-2511
614-464-4099 • E-mail cofmuseum@aol.com
Antique fire equipment, Junior Fire Academy. Open Tues.–Sat. 10 a.m.–4 p.m., closed Sunday and Monday. Group tours by appointment. Adults $4, seniors $3, children 6 and up $2; children under 6 free. Call for special group rates.

The Strand Theatre
28 East Winter Street
Delaware, OH 43015
740-363-4914 • www.thestrandtheatre.net
Call for movies and times.

Green Lawn Cemetery
1000 Greenlawn Avenue
Columbus, OH 43223
The resting place of many of Columbus' best-known citizens, including James Thurber and the Goodale, Deshler and Battelle families. The

original chapel was designed by Frank Packard, who also designed the Seneca Hotel, the old Memorial Hall on East Broad Street, and many landmark churches and homes in Columbus. The cemetery also features several beautiful family mausoleums and impressive statuary (including one marker featuring the deceased, Emil Ambos, at life size wearing his favorite fishing clothes). Please remember that under Ohio law, cemeteries close at dusk.

Perkins Observatory

P.O. Box 449
Delaware, OH 43015
Located on the east side of U.S. Route 23 about 10 miles north of I-270
740-363-1257 • http://www.perkins-observatory.org/
Features public programs on most Friday and Saturday evenings through-out the year. Admission $6 for adults, $4 for seniors and children when purchased in advance; add one dollar for tickets purchased the day of the program. Call or visit the Perkins Web site for schedules and more infor-mation. Advance reservations are strongly suggested.

Orton Hall/Orton Geological Museum

155 South Oval Mall
The Ohio State University
Columbus, OH 43210
(614) 292-6896
The Orton Geological Museum is normally open Mon.–Fri. 9 a.m.–5 p.m.; it is best to call before visiting. Visits at other times can by arranged by appointment. Admission is free. Exhibits include the skeleton of a giant ground sloth — one of four found in Ohio — meteorites, rocks, minerals and dinosaurs, including a scale model of a *Tyrannosaurus rex* head.

More Ghosts and Columbus History

Want to find out more? Check these sources to start.

Ghost Books

● Chris Woodyard is the maven of Ohio ghost stories.

Woodyard, Chris. *The Ghost Hunter's Guide to Haunted Ohio.* Kestrel Publications, Dayton, OH, 2000.

Woodyard, Chris. *Haunted Ohio: Ghostly Tales from the Buckeye State.* Kestrel Publications, Dayton, OH, 1991.

Woodyard, Chris. *Haunted Ohio II: More Ghostly Tales from the Buckeye State.* Kestrel Publications, Dayton, OH, 1992.

Woodyard, Chris. *Haunted Ohio III: Still More Ghostly Tales from the Buckeye State.* Kestrel Publications, Dayton, OH, 1994.

Woodyard, Chris. *Haunted Ohio IV: Restless Spirits.* Kestrel Publications, Dayton, OH, 1997.

Woodyard, Chris. *Spooky Ohio: 13 Traditional Tales.* Kestrel Publications, Dayton, OH, 1995.

● Connie Cartmell weaves spooky tales from Marietta, the oldest permanent settlement in the old Northwest Territory.

Cartmell, Connie. *Ghosts of Marietta.* © 1996 by Connie Cartmell. Published by River Press and Connie Cartmell, 1996.

● Anne Oscard brings together female ghosts from the tri-state area.

Oscard, Anne. *Tristate Terrors.* ©1996 by Anne Oscard. Hermit Publications, Dayton, OH.

● Michael Norman and Beth Scott produced a number of good collections of ghost stories. This is their midwest collection.

Norman, Michael and Beth Scott. *Haunted Heartland.* Stanton & Lee, Madison, WI, © 1985.

Web Sites

- *Forgotten Ohio* • www.forgottenoh.com

  This site has Ohio ghost stories as well as sections on Ohio cemeteries, abandoned buildings and structures, and ghost towns.*

- *The Ghosts of Ohio* • http://www.ghostsofohio.org/goo.htm

  Lots of Ohio and nearby ghost stories. The Ghosts of Ohio is actually a not-for-profit group which was formed for the purpose of investigating ghosts scientifically. They are NOT "ghostbusters," but will investigate alleged hauntings.

- *Ghosts of the Prairie* • www.prairieghosts.com

  The site of the American Ghost Society; ghost stories from all over, plus extensive information on ghost hunting. Also features an enormous catalog of ghost books from just about everywhere.

- *Invisible Ink: Books on Ghosts and Hauntings*™ • www.invink.com

  Chris Woodyard's site features a large catalog of books as well as lots of general information about ghosts.

Please note that neither the author of Columbus Ghosts *nor Emuses encourages or condones illegal trespassing. However, this site is included for its truly fascinating content and historical information about several haunted sites.*

Columbus History Books

Arter, Bill. *Columbus Vignettes*, vols. 1–6. Nida-Eckstein Printing, Inc., Columbus, OH.

Cole, Charles C. Jr. *A Fragile Capital: Identity and the Early Years of Columbus, Ohio.* Ohio State University Press, Columbus, Ohio, 2001.

Henderson, Andrew. *Forgotten Columbus.* Copyright © 2002 by Andrew Henderson. Arcadia Press, an imprint of Tempus Publishing, Chicago, IL.

Lentz, Ed. *As It Were: Stories of Old Columbus.* Red Mountain Press 1998.

Lentz, Ed. *As It Were: Stories of Old Columbus, vol. 2.* Red Mountain Press, 2001.

Thomas, Robert D., ed. *Columbus Unforgettables: A Collection of Columbus Yesterdays and Todays.* Robert D. Thomas, 1983.

Thomas, Robert D., ed. *More Columbus Unforgettables: A Further Collection of Columbus Yesterdays and Todays.* Robert D. Thomas, 1986.

Libraries and Archives

The Columbus Metropolitan Library (Main Library)
  96 South Grant Street • www.columbuslibrary.org
  614-645-2275 (general) • 614-645-2710 (Biography, History & Travel)

The Ohio Historical Society Archives/Library
  I-71 and 17th Avenue (in the Ohio Historical Center)
  http://www.ohiohistory.org/resource/archlib/index.html
  614-297-2510

The Ohio State University
William Oxley Thompson Memorial Library
  1858 Neil Avenue Mall
  www.lib.ohio-state.edu/Lib_Info/MAIN.html
  614-292-6154

The Ohio State University Archives
  2700 Kenny Rd. • www.lib.ohio-state.edu/arvweb/
  614-292-2409 • 614-292-1767 (Photo Archives)

The State Library of Ohio
  274 East First Avenue • http://winslo.state.oh.us/
  614-644-7061

Index

About the Author

Writer and designer Robin Smith has been collecting ghost stories since she was eleven years old; her first book of Columbus tales, *Columbus Ghosts: Historical Haunts of Ohio's Capital*, was published in 2002. A lifelong resident of Ohio and a former *Ohio Magazine* staffer, she has collected a large number of stories and tons of Ohio trivia with which she torments her family and friends. She lives in the Columbus area with her husband Brian and daughter Jessica.

About the Publisher

Emuses was founded in December 2000 by writer and editor Jennifer E. Poleon and designers Kathy Murphy and Robin Smith. We specialize in publication design, including books, magazines and newsletters.
Write us at

Emuses
P.O. Box 1264
Worthington, OH 43085-1264

or e-mail us at

emuses@columbus.rr.com

Pass the shivers on!

Columbus Ghosts II: More Central Ohio Haunts

Order additional copies to share with friends!

And don't forget

Columbus Ghosts: Historical Haunts of Ohio's Capital

Just send this form with a check or money order
(payable to Emuses) to
Emuses, P.O. Box 1264, Worthington, OH 43085

Title	Qty.	Price per book	Total
Columbus Ghosts II: More Central Ohio Haunts		$13.95	
Columbus Ghosts: Historical Haunts of Ohio's Capital		$13.95	
Ohio residents add $.94 per book sales tax			
Shipping/handling add $4.95 (up to 5 books)			
TOTAL ENCLOSED			

*For more than five books or to order books for resale
please call 614-529-9454.*

Name

Address

City/State/Zip

Phone   Email

*Have a ghost story you'd like to share? Contact us at
ColumbusHaunts@aol.com!*